baby and toddler
Meal
planner

Nicola Graimes

p

This is a Parragon Book
This edition published in 2006

Parragon
Queen Street House
4 Queen Street
Bath, BA1 1HE, UK

Copyright © Parragon Books Ltd 2001
Updated 2003

Produced by:
The Bridgewater Book Company Ltd

Cover by Talking Design

ISBN 1-40547-575-7
Printed in China

Contents

FIVE TO SIX MONTHS

Weaning is the gradual process of reducing a baby's total dependence on milk to eating a full and varied diet, eventually the same as the rest of the family. However daunting this may first sound, the process of introducing so-called 'solids' – actually purées – is in fact very simple. The most important piece of advice is relax and don't rush into it because of family or peer pressure. Remember, food should be one of life's pleasures.

Introduction

Having a baby is a bit like being on a rollercoaster; no sooner have you mastered (or at least become accustomed to) breast or bottle feeding, than it's time to tackle a new stage in your baby's development – weaning. I can remember feeling distinctly nervy about the prospect of introducing solids to my daughter's diet.

What to feed and when are the two main concerns of parents. Up until quite recently it was usual for parents to begin weaning at four months. Now new Department of Health guidelines recommend there is no nutritional benefit to introducing solids before a baby is six months old and breastfeeding is the best form of nutrition for babies up until this age. Many quite ordinary foods can cause allergies, and most babies' digestive systems are unable to cope with anything more than breast or formula milk before 5–6 months. For those parents who feel their baby is ready for solids in the fifth month, I have included a general weaning chart on page 10. These solids should be regarded as simply a taster of what's to come and as a supplement to breast or formula milk. Only introduce solids when your baby is sitting up properly and has begun to exercise some control over his or her tongue.

ABOVE *Introduce a new food a spoon at a time – this way, it is much more manageable for your child.*

The aim of this book is to ease any anxieties you may have, as well as smooth the path from your baby's first taste of solids to his or her participating in family meals. The advice is designed to be practical and reassuring, to help you give your baby the best start in life. Many parents feel that they don't have the required time or cookery skills to make home-made baby foods, but first foods couldn't be easier to make and, especially if prepared in bulk, take the minimum amount of time. By making your own foods you can also familiarise your baby with a wide range of tastes and textures.

Every baby and toddler is different, with his or her own particular likes and dislikes, which can sometimes change on a daily basis. It wasn't unusual for my daughter to absolutely adore a particular food to the extent she couldn't eat enough of it, then to turn up her nose the next time she was offered it. Most parents will vouch that this behaviour is common. However perturbed or frustrated you may feel, it is counter-productive to force your baby to eat and can lead to mealtimes becoming a type of power game. Many parents recall times when their child ate nothing but toast for weeks without any adverse effects, which is reassuring.

ABOVE *Try not to worry too much about weaning: if you are relaxed, then your baby will be too.*

Is Your Baby Ready?

Your baby is ready to take his or her first spoonful from age five to six months. Experts agree that a baby's digestive system is too immature for solids before this age, and early weaning can put stress on the kidneys, as well as trigger possible allergies. Breast or formula milk provides all the nutrients a baby needs for the first six months.

All babies are different and progress at their own pace, but the following may indicate that your baby is ready for solids:
• starts waking in the night, after initially sleeping through
• seems unsatisfied after a milk feed and hungrier than usual
• starts to demand more frequent feeds and shows an interest in your food

Weaning guidelines

It is worth reiterating that milk provides everything nutritionally your baby requires for the first six months. You may wish to introduce a little taster of solids in the fifth month if you feel your baby is ready to sample baby rice or a simple fruit or vegetable purée, but it is advisable to hold off offering solids for as long as possible.

• Don't force feed your baby: eating is a new skill, which must be accomplished gradually. Your baby is exercising previously unused muscles and will initially try to suck food, which explains why it is often pushed right out of the mouth or appears to be 'spat' out.

• Be scrupulous with hygiene: make sure all spoons and bowls are sterilised and don't store any leftover food for later use.

• Choose the right time to introduce solids: it's important to pick a time when you're not rushed and your baby is not feeling too tired or hungry – the middle of the day is often seen as the best option for both of you. It may be a good idea to give your baby a little milk first to curb any hunger pangs, but as feeding becomes established, start to offer food before milk.

• Face-to-face interaction is important: try to be as encouraging as possible.

ABOVE *If you are relaxed when you are feeding your baby, he or she will be comfortable with the idea too.*

First foods

To begin, offer a little baby rice or a fruit or vegetable purée (see recipe section) on the tip of a shallow plastic spoon or your finger. Commercial baby rice is readily available but it is also simple and quick to prepare your own, and then freeze it in convenient-sized portions. Don't expect your baby to eat more than a tablespoon or even less – at this stage, the amount that is eaten by your child is immaterial.

For the first three weeks, offer the same food for around three days at a time to enable your baby to get used to new tastes and for you to gauge if there is any form of allergic reaction. Thin and runny single-ingredient purées made from fairly mild-tasting fruits and vegetables such as potatoes, carrots, apples and bananas are generally best. Wash the fruit or vegetables thoroughly and peel them, removing any core or pips. By the fourth or fifth week, and if your baby is happily accepting the food that you are offering him or her, you can start to increase the number of solid feeds from one to three a day. Water or diluted fruit juice can now replace the lunchtime milk feed. Again, introduce new foods gradually and if a new food is rejected don't try it again for a few days or, alternatively, combine it with baby rice or another type of purée to disguise it.

What do Babies Need?

While the saying 'you are what you eat' may be an overused cliché, it's not far from the truth. Health experts now suggest that what we eat in childhood has implications for our future health. Consequently, it's crucial for parents to encourage their child to enjoy a varied diet as soon as possible.

Breast, formula and cow's milk

For the first six months of your baby's life, breast (or formula) milk provides all the nutrients and nourishment he or she needs for growth and development. Breast (or formula) milk should form a major part of his or her life up until a year old, when cow's milk can be introduced as a drink.

Experts firmly believe that breast milk is best for a baby, since it provides the correct balance of vitamins, minerals and fats in a readily digestible form. Breast milk contains the antibodies necessary to help fight off infections, and research shows that it may also improve mental development in the long term.

At some stage you may wish to introduce a bottle for at least some of the milk feeds if, for instance, you are returning to work. This transition will take time, so be patient with yourself and your baby.

Breads, cereals and potatoes

Otherwise known as starchy foods, breads, cereals and potatoes are an excellent source of energy, vitamins, minerals and fibre. These foods along with pasta, rice and low-sugar breakfast cereals should form a major part of the diet. Do not give wheat-based foods to babies under six months.

Fruit and vegetables

Fresh and frozen, and to a lesser extent canned, fruit and vegetables are an essential part of a baby's diet. They are perfect first foods, providing rich amounts of vitamins, minerals and fibre. From six months, try to give at least four to five different types of fresh produce a day to your baby.

Meat, fish, eggs and vegetarian alternatives

These are a good source of protein, essential for growth and repair. Your child should be given a protein food at every meal but it is vital to offer a good variety, including beans, lentils and soya-based foods.

Dairy foods

Milk, cheese and yogurt provide protein, vitamins and minerals, particularly calcium, for healthy bones and teeth. Cow's milk can be used in cooking from six months, but is not to be given as a drink before a year old, when full-cream milk can be introduced. Skimmed cow's milk is not recommended before your child is five years old, since it lacks the energy a growing child requires.

Sweet foods

Babies seem to have a naturally sweet tooth and the sweetness of breast milk may be partly to blame. There's nothing wrong with the occasional sweet treat but sugar can rot the teeth and lead to obesity.

Salty foods

Don't add salt to food for babies and young children as their kidneys are insufficiently mature to cope. If you are cooking for the whole family, separate your child's portion before adding any seasoning. Salt is added to many commercial foods, and to stocks and yeast-based spreads too.

IRON Babies are born with a store of iron and the mineral is also found in breast and formula milk. However, by about six months, most babies have used up their iron reserves and even if they are drinking iron-fortified milk, it is important to include foods rich in the mineral in their diet. Good sources include: red meat, liver, fish, eggs, beans and lentils, leafy green vegetables, wholegrain cereals, fortified breakfast cereals and dried fruit, especially apricots.

Cooking for your Baby

Ideally, every morsel that passes your baby's lips should be home-prepared, but this is unrealistic for most of us. Having said this, it's vital to provide as much fresh, unprocessed food as possible, and the recipes in this book have been created to help even the busiest parent. They don't require hours of preparation or slaving over a hot stove and most are suitable for home freezing.

Fresh is best

Many of us fall into the trap of believing our little ones prefer so-called 'children's food', and pander to our expectations by buying foods that we would not normally even contemplate. Experts firmly believe that good eating habits are formed early, so it's important for parents to provide a variety of foods, encompassing a whole different range of flavours, colours and textures. I was certainly surprised to find that my daughter loved foods that were strongly flavoured and quite highly spiced, especially curries and anything that contained onion and garlic.

Commercial foods

Lack of time and energy leads many of us to resort to the easy option. However, now is not the time to feel guilty – the occasional packet or jar will not harm a baby's health, but relying on them 100 per cent might. When buying commercial baby foods, it is advisable to check the label for unwanted additives, sugars (sucrose, dextrose, glucose), artificial sweeteners, salt and thickeners such as modified starch, which simply bulk out ingredients. Instead opt for brands – especially the organic ones – that are free from additives and are without added salt, sugar and sweeteners.

Allergies

It has been suggested that the number of children with food intolerances is on the increase, yet it is also true that life-threatening allergies are extremely rare.

ABOVE *Becoming more aware of what's in the food you eat can help you shop more healthily.*

In children the most commonly responsible foods are cow's milk, gluten, eggs, seafood, peanuts, tomatoes, sugar and strawberries, with symptoms ranging from rashes, upset stomachs and hyperactivity to asthma, eczema, breathing difficulties and swelling of the throat. If you have a history of food allergies in the family or suspect a problem with a particular food and are very concerned, it is advisable to talk to your health visitor or doctor.

First Foods

A common question from new mothers is 'When can I introduce certain foods?' The following list is a good starting point but is not exhaustive. Use this chart as a guide, adapting it according to what is in season and what you are preparing for your family at the time.

DRINKS

Generally babies under 6 months do not need additional drinks but if your baby is thirsty between feeds, offer cooled, boiled water rather than sugary drinks. There are many commercial baby drinks available but most of them, including herbal ones, are laden with sugar. Artificial sweeteners are no better since they can upset the stomach. If you do offer your baby fruit juice, it is advisable to dilute it with water (1 part juice to 5 parts water). Offer drinks in a feeder cup or beaker rather than a bottle from six months to avoid the risk of dental decay.

Suitable drinks breast, formula or follow-on milk, water, very dilute, unsweetened fruit juice.

Unsuitable drinks sweetened fruit juice, squash, drinks with artificial sweeteners, tea, coffee, cola and other fizzy drinks, alcohol.

WEANING CHART

FOODS	DRINKS	SHOPPING LIST	FOODS TO AVOID
5-6 MONTHS			
Smooth purées.	Breast or formula milk – about five feeds a day.	Short-grain white rice, apples, bananas, pears, potatoes, carrots, sweet potatoes, courgettes. Thin porridge can be made from cornmeal, sago, millet, avocado, mango, melon, dried apricots, prunes, pears, peaches, broccoli, peas, cauliflower, leeks, apricots, swede, spinach, French beans, parsnips and squash.	Salt, sugar, honey, berries, dairy foods, eggs, meat, fish and shellfish, citrus fruit, wheat-based foods and those containing gluten, nuts, fatty foods, spices and chilli.
6-9 MONTHS			
Six to eight months: coarsely puréed food. **Eight to nine months:** mashed or minced foods.	Breast, formula or follow-on milk – about four feeds a day, cooled boiled water, diluted unsweetened fruit juice (1 part juice: 5 parts water).	Fruits, vegetables, dairy products such as fromage frais, cheese, yogurt and milk puddings, cow's milk (use in cooking), wheat, eggs (well-cooked), smooth peanut butter, lentils, beans, chicken, meat and fish.	Cow's milk (as a drink), whole nuts, shellfish, soft or blue cheese, chillies, salt, honey, spices, raw eggs and sugar.
9-12 MONTHS			
Chopped foods.	Breast, formula or follow-on milk – about three feeds a day, cooled boiled water, diluted unsweetened fruit juice (1 part juice: 5 parts water).	Fruits, vegetables, meat, chicken, fish, dairy products such as cheese, yogurt and milk puddings, wheat, eggs, smooth peanut butter.	Raw eggs, shellfish, whole nuts, honey, chillies, salt, cow's milk as a drink, soft and blue cheese.
12-18 MONTHS			
Chopped foods.	Breast, formula or follow-on milk – about two feeds a day, cooled boiled water, diluted unsweetened fruit juice (1 part juice: 5 parts water).	Same as family.	Whole nuts, chillies, shellfish and raw eggs.

MEAL PLANNER 1

5–6 MONTHS	EARLY MORNING	BREAKFAST	LUNCH	TEA	BEDTIME
WEEK 1					
Days 1–7	Milk	Milk	Baby rice, milk	Milk	Milk
WEEK 2					
Days 1–4	Milk	Milk	Apple purée, milk	Milk	Milk
Days 4–7	Milk	Milk	Carrot purée, milk	Milk	Milk
WEEK THREE					
Days 1–3	Milk	Banana purée, milk	Milk	Carrot purée, milk	Milk
Days 3–5	Milk	Apple purée, milk	Milk	Potato purée, milk	Milk
Days 5–7	Milk	Pear purée, milk	Milk	Sweet potato purée, milk	Milk
WEEK FOUR					
Day 1	Milk	Apple purée, milk	Courgette purée, milk	Sweet potato purée, milk	Milk
Day 2	Milk	Apple purée, milk	Courgette purée, milk	Carrot purée, milk	Milk
Day 3	Milk	Baby rice, milk	Banana purée, milk	Carrot purée, milk	Milk
Day 4	Milk	Baby rice, milk	Banana purée, milk	Potato purée, milk	Milk
Day 5	Milk	Pear purée, baby rice	Carrot purée, milk	Potato purée, milk	Milk
Day 6	Milk	Pear purée, baby rice	Carrot purée, milk	Apple purée, milk	Milk
Day 7	Milk	Banana purée, baby rice	Sweet potato purée, milk	Courgette purée, milk	Milk

The above meal planner is a general guide to the gradual introduction of solids for a baby of five to six months, since some parents may feel their baby is ready to sample some simple foods in the fifth month. If you wish to delay weaning until six months, as now recommended by the Department of Health, it is advisable you introduce a wider range of foods at this age to include yogurt, fromage frais, chicken, well-cooked eggs and wheat. Introduce these foods on a gradual basis to allow your baby's digestive system to adjust to solids.

Baby Rice

PREPARATION TIME: 3 MINUTES	**COOKING TIME:** 20–25 MINUTES
FREEZING: SUITABLE	**SERVES:** 15 PORTIONS

Baby rice is a good introduction to solid foods and can be mixed with breast or formula milk to make a runny purée. There are many commercial versions of baby rice around but it is just as easy to make at home. Admittedly, home-made baby rice is not fortified with extra vitamins, but your baby will be getting nutrients from breast or formula milk.

❶ Rinse the rice under cold running water. Put the rice into a saucepan and add enough cold water to just cover it. Bring to the boil, stir, then reduce the heat. Cover the pan and simmer for 20–25 minutes, until the water has been absorbed and the grains are very tender.

❷ Purée the rice in a blender with breast or formula milk until smooth.

> **INGREDIENTS:**
>
> 40 g/1½ oz white short-grain rice

TIP Baby rice makes an ideal base for any fruit or vegetable purée and is a simple and easy way of introducing your baby to new tastes and textures. Apple or pear work particularly well with baby rice. If using frozen baby rice, make sure it has completely defrosted and is heated through thoroughly beforehand.

Pear Purée

PREPARATION TIME: 2 MINUTES	**COOKING TIME:** 5–8 MINUTES
FREEZING: SUITABLE	**SERVES:** 2–3 PORTIONS

It is unnecessary to cook pears after your baby is 6 months old but, prior to this, cooking is advisable to make the fruit easier to digest.

❶ Wash, peel, core and chop the pear. Put the pear into a saucepan with the water. Bring to the boil and cook for 5–8 minutes, until the fruit is tender.

❷ Purée the pear in a blender until smooth, adding a little of the cooking water if necessary.

> **INGREDIENTS:**
>
> 1 small ripe pear
>
> 2 tbsp water

VARIATION Apple can be cooked and puréed in the same way as pear for a digestible purée. Apple is often the most popular fruit!

Fruit and Vegetable Purées

These basic fruit and vegetable purées make perfect first foods for your baby. I have intentionally kept them simple to enable him or her to become accustomed to eating solids and tasting new flavours. In time, the purées can be combined to make a wider choice of taste variations. The portion sizes given are a rough guide. You will find that your baby will eat no more than a few teaspoons at first – if that. Store the remainder in the fridge for use the next day or double up the quantity given and freeze.

Carrot Purée

PREPARATION TIME: 2 MINUTES COOKING TIME: 10–15 MINUTES
FREEZING: SUITABLE   SERVES: 1–2

The natural sweetness of carrots makes this purée a popular first food. Pick small, young, preferably organic vegetables.

❶ Scrape or peel the carrot, then slice. Put the carrot into a saucepan with the water. Bring to the boil and cook for 10–15 minutes.

INGREDIENTS:
1 small carrot
2 tbsp water

❷ Purée the carrot in a blender until smooth, adding a little of the cooking water if necessary.

Courgette Purée

PREPARATION TIME: 2 MINUTES COOKING TIME: 4–5 MINUTES
FREEZING: SUITABLE   SERVES: 2 PORTIONS

Courgette can be a difficult vegetable to introduce to your child, so it is best to offer it at as young an age as possible. It can be combined with potato to make it more palatable.

❶ Trim and slice the courgette – there is no need to peel it. Steam or boil the courgette for 4–5 minutes, until tender.

INGREDIENTS:
1 medium courgette
2 tbsp water

❷ Purée in a blender until smooth or mash with a fork.

VARIATION Potato and sweet potato purées can be a useful base for other vegetables. Cut a whole potato into small cubes. Bring a pan of water to the boil and cook the potato for 15–20 minutes until tender. Purée with breast or formula milk until smooth and creamy.

Avocado Purée

PREPARATION TIME: 2 MINUTES

FREEZING: UNSUITABLE   **SERVES:** 1 PORTION

Choose ripe, unblemished fruit for this purée and prepare just before serving because avocado flesh discolours very quickly after it has been cut.

❶ Peel and stone the avocado and scoop out the flesh with a spoon. Mash the avocado with a fork until smooth and creamy.

❷ Serve immediately before the flesh browns and discolours.

INGREDIENTS:

½ small avocado

TIP Squeeze fresh lemon juice over the unused avocado half to prevent the flesh discolouring. The avocado can then be kept in the refrigerator for use the following day.

Mango Purée

PREPARATION TIME: 2 MINUTES   **COOKING TIME:** 2 MINUTES

FREEZING: SUITABLE   **SERVES:** 2–3 PORTIONS

Mangoes are loved by babies, as they are naturally sweet and easy to digest. They are also a good introduction to the more 'tropical' kinds of fruit available. Do make sure the mango is ripe before you use it – unripe fruit can upset small stomachs. You can steam the mango if you need to.

❶ Wash, peel, stone and slice the mango. Steam for 2 minutes or, if very ripe, mash with a fork or pass through a sieve until smooth to remove the fibres.

INGREDIENTS:

1 small ripe mango

Melon Purée

PREPARATION TIME: 2 MINUTES **COOKING TIME:** 2 MINUTES
FREEZING: UNSUITABLE **SERVES:** 1-2 PORTIONS

Any variety of melon can be given uncooked to babies as long as it's sweet and juicy. It may be necessary to steam the fruit if it's not entirely ripe. Galia, Charentais and Cantaloupe melons tend to have the sweetest flesh.

❶ Peel the melon then remove any seeds before chopping it. Mash with a fork or pass through a sieve until smooth.

❷ Alternatively, steam for 2 minutes, until tender, and mash with a fork until smooth.

INGREDIENTS:
1 wedge of melon

VARIATION A banana can be mashed in the same way as a melon for a tasty purée. Be sure to use ripe fruit.

Dried Apricot Purée

PREPARATION TIME: 2 MINUTES, PLUS OVERNIGHT SOAKING
COOKING TIME: 10–15 MINUTES **FREEZING:** SUITABLE **SERVES:** 3–5 PORTIONS

Dried apricots are a good source of iron and beta-carotene but must be soaked overnight to make them easier to eat. Like other dried fruits, apricots have a laxative effect so it's important that they are given in small amounts. Other dried fruit such as prunes, apples, pears and peaches are good too.

❶ Wash and soak the apricots in cold water overnight. The next day, drain the apricots and place in a saucepan.

INGREDIENTS:
8 unsulphured, dried, ready-to-eat apricots

❷ Cover with water and bring to the boil, then reduce the heat and simmer for 10–15 minutes, until soft. Purée in a blender until smooth, adding a little of the cooking water if necessary.

Orchard Fruit Purée

PREPARATION TIME: 4 MINUTES	COOKING TIME: 5 MINUTES
FREEZING: SUITABLE	SERVES: 6–8 PORTIONS

A firm favourite with little ones. It also makes a delicious accompaniment to roasts and vegetarian alternatives.

❶ Wash, peel, core or stone the fruit, then chop into small pieces. Steam or boil the apple and pear for 5 minutes, or until soft.

❷ Purée the apple and pear with the peach in a blender until smooth, adding a little of the cooking water if necessary.

INGREDIENTS:
1 small dessert apple
1 small ripe pear
1 small ripe peach

Broccoli & Pea Purée

PREPARATION TIME: 2 MINUTES	COOKING TIME: 5–6 MINUTES
FREEZING: SUITABLE	SERVES: 2–3 PORTIONS

A vibrant combination that is full of goodness. This bright green purée is certainly a colourful dish!

❶ Steam or boil the broccoli for 8–10 minutes, adding the peas 5 minutes before the end of the cooking time.

❷ Purée the broccoli and peas in a blender until smooth, adding a little of the cooking water if necessary.

INGREDIENTS:
3 florets broccoli
handful of frozen peas

Cauliflower, Potato & Leek Purée

PREPARATION TIME: 3 MINUTES	COOKING TIME: 15–20 MINUTES
FREEZING: SUITABLE	SERVES: 4–6 PORTIONS

Introducing potential 'problem' vegetables at an early age can cut down on fussy eating when your child gets older. This combination also works well with broccoli and sweet potato.

❶ Wash, peel and cube the potato. Wash the leek, remove the tough outer layer, then slice thinly. Steam or boil the potato, cauliflower and leek for 15–20 minutes, until tender.

❷ Purée in a blender with a little breast or formula milk until smooth and creamy.

INGREDIENTS:
1 medium potato
3 florets cauliflower
½ small leek

Apricot & Swede Purée

PREPARATION TIME: 3 MINUTES	COOKING TIME: 15–20 MINUTES
FREEZING: SUITABLE	SERVES: 2–3 PORTIONS

It is a good idea to encourage your baby to try a range of fruit and vegetable combinations in the hope that your child will not be a fussy eater in the future – well, that's the theory!

❶ Wash, peel and cube the wedge of swede. Halve the apricots and then stone them carefully. Steam or boil the swede for 15–20 minutes until tender, adding the apricots 5 minutes before the end of the cooking time.

❷ Sieve to remove the apricot skin and purée in a blender until smooth, adding a little of the cooking water if necessary.

INGREDIENTS:
1 wedge of swede
2 fresh ripe apricots

Spinach & French Bean Purée

PREPARATION TIME: 3 MINUTES	COOKING TIME: 8 MINUTES
FREEZING: SUITABLE	SERVES: 3–4 PORTIONS

From around 6 months of age, your baby's natural iron stores begin to deplete and it is vital at this stage to introduce foods that provide this mineral. Spinach is a good source of iron, which is more readily absorbed if it is served with a cup of very dilute fresh orange juice.

❶ Wash, trim and slice the beans. Wash the spinach and remove any coarse stalks. Steam or boil the beans for 8 minutes. Steam the spinach for 5 minutes, until tender and wilted, then squeeze out any excess water.

❷ Purée in a blender until smooth, adding a little of the cooking water.

INGREDIENTS:
3 French beans
40 g/1½ oz fresh young spinach leaves

Apple, Parsnip & Butternut Squash Purée

PREPARATION TIME: 3 MINUTES	COOKING TIME: 15 MINUTES
FREEZING: SUITABLE	SERVES: 3–4 PORTIONS

Butternut squash is a good source of vitamin C and, when puréed, makes a nourishing meal.

❶ Wash, peel and dice the parsnip and squash. Wash, peel, core and chop the apple. Place the parsnip and squash in a saucepan and cover with water. Bring to the boil and cook the parsnip and squash for 15 minutes until tender, adding the apple 5 minutes before the end of the cooking time.

INGREDIENTS:
1 small parsnip
1 small wedge of butternut squash
1 small dessert apple

❷ Purée the apple, parsnip and butternut squash in a blender until smooth, adding a little of the cooking water if necessary.

SIX TO NINE MONTHS

During this period you'll notice a change in your baby. He or she will probably begin to cut a few teeth and will start to sit up, first in a bouncy chair, or propped up, and finally progressing to a high chair. This increasing independence is also shown in your baby's eating habits. He or she will enjoy using his or her hands and eating finger foods. A much wider variety of foods may now be offered, including those rich in protein. Plenty of bibs are a necessity!

Making Food Fun

Once your baby is happy with his or her first foods, it is time to introduce a wider range of fruits and vegetables, as well as protein foods such as lean meat, white fish, cottage cheese, yogurt and well-cooked eggs. Health practitioners call this the second stage of weaning.

ABOVE *Fresh fruit is a great favourite with babies – the larger and juicier the better!*

New tastes

Although milk will still form an important part of your baby's diet, it no longer provides all the necessary nutrients. If your baby is happily taking solids, you'll probably find that he or she can now eat many family meals, but avoid highly spiced or seasoned foods. It is a good idea to remove a baby-sized portion of what you are eating before seasoning the remainder of the meal.

At this stage, it's a good idea to familiarise your baby with a wider range of flavours and you will definitely reap the benefits in the future. New government guidelines suggest introducing fish and hard cheese from six to nine months, while chicken, meat and beans and lentils are fine from six months. These foods combine well with other foods, especially those with stronger flavours, have a pleasing texture and take little time to prepare. Mash beans and lentils well and only use in small quantities, since they can be difficult to digest.

Fromage frais and yogurt lend themselves to many types of dishes and add a delicious creaminess to pasta sauces, soups and stews. Eggs must be well cooked and mashed or finely chopped to avoid choking. Pasta, potatoes and bread are great favourites with children and are versatile.

From six months, your baby's iron stores start to deplete, so it is important to include sources of iron (see page 7) in his or her diet. Vitamin C-rich foods and drinks can enhance iron absorption and it is a good idea to offer them at the same time for the best effect.

Babies love fruit – citrus fruit, strawberries and mango can now be included, although it is wise to limit the quantities as they can be acidic on the stomach, and berries can be a source of allergies.

Three meals a day

There are no hard and fast rules when it comes to how much your baby should eat, but the general guideline is 1–4 tablespoons of food per mealtime – don't panic if your baby eats more or less than this. Babies seem to thrive on routine and therefore it is a good idea to introduce three meals a day. You will have a less fussy eater if you now move on from purées to mashed or minced food.

Milk and drinks

You'll find that as your baby's appetite increases, his or her need for milk will decline. He or she should still be drinking 600 ml/1 pint of breast, formula or follow-on milk each day, but once solid feeding is established, it is advisable to stop giving milk at mealtimes because it can depress the appetite. Avoid giving cow's milk as a drink, although it is now suitable for cooking. Instead, give cooled boiled water or very weak unsweetened fruit juice.

Finger foods

Fingers foods help to comfort sore gums and also give your baby a chance to use his or her hands and practise chewing. Steamed sticks of carrot, baby sweetcorn, mangetout and pepper are popular, as are peeled chunks of apple, pear, banana, melon and papaya.

MEAL PLANNER 2

6–9 MONTHS	EARLY MORNING	BREAKFAST	MID-MORNING	LUNCH	MID-AFTERNOON	TEA	BEDTIME
		(with diluted unsweetened fruit juice – 1 part juice: 5 parts water – or cooled boiled water)		(same drink as breakfast)		(same drink as lunch)	
Day 1	Milk	Apricot porridge	Milk	Carrot, bean & swede purée Pear purée	Milk	Avocado purée & toast fingers Banana yogurt custard	Milk
Day 2	Milk	Weetabix & banana purée	Milk	Spring vegetable risotto Fromage frais & mango purée	Milk	Houmus with crudités Pitta bread Apricot porridge	Milk
Day 3	Milk	Fromage frais & mango purée Toast fingers	Milk	Cauliflower, potato & leek purée Sunset jelly	Milk	Tuna salad Apple & plum yogurt	Milk
Day 4	Milk	Ready Brek & pear purée	Milk	Apple, parsnip & butternut squash purée Fromage frais & apricot purée	Milk	Chicken & pineapple cheese Breadsticks Sunset jelly	Milk
Day 5	Milk	Apricot porridge	Milk	Baked plaice with tomato rice Pear purée	Milk	Pastina Banana yogurt custard	Milk
Day 6	Milk	Baby cereal & pear purée	Milk	Oaty vegetable purée Melon purée	Milk	Bean & root vegetable mash Fromage frais & mango purée	Milk
Day 7	Milk	Weetabix & banana purée	Milk	Minestrone soup Toast fingers Orchard fruit purée	Milk	Tuna salad Apple & plum yogurt	Milk

Oaty Vegetable Purée

PREPARATION TIME: 5 MINUTES **COOKING TIME:** 20 MINUTES

FREEZING: SUITABLE **SERVES:** 4–6 PORTIONS

The addition of oats to this wholesome purée means there is plenty of substance – something for your baby to use new teeth on! This purée also introduces tomato to your child's diet.

❶ Put the oats into a saucepan, cover with half water and half milk and bring to the boil. Reduce the heat and simmer, stirring occasionally, for 4–5 minutes, until the grains are soft and creamy.

❷ Meanwhile, steam the leek for 10–15 minutes, until tender. Combine the leek with the oats, sweetcorn, tomato and butter in a small saucepan and stir until heated through. Purée or mash, depending on the desired consistency. (You may need to add a little extra breast, formula or cow's milk.)

INGREDIENTS:
2 tbsp porridge oats
1 small leek, finely chopped
2 tbsp canned sweetcorn, drained and rinsed
1 medium tomato, skinned, seeded and chopped
small knob of unsalted butter or margarine

VARIATION Carrot, French bean and swede cooked and puréed is a tasty combination.

Minestrone Soup

PREPARATION TIME: 10 MINUTES **COOKING TIME:** 35 MINUTES

FREEZING: SUITABLE **SERVES:** 4 PORTIONS

This classic Italian soup is a nutritious combination of beans, pasta and vegetables, providing a good range of vitamins.

❶ Heat the olive oil in a heavy-based saucepan. Add the onion and carrot and cook over a medium heat for 8–10 minutes, stirring occasionally, until the vegetables have softened.

❷ Add the bay leaf, stock and passata, then bring to the boil. Reduce the heat, cover, and simmer for 15 minutes, or until the vegetables are tender.

❸ Add the pasta and beans, then bring the soup back to the boil and simmer until the pasta is tender. Stir occasionally to prevent the pasta sticking to the bottom.

INGREDIENTS:
1 tbsp olive oil
½ small onion, finely chopped
1 small carrot, peeled and diced
1 bay leaf
300 ml/½ pint no-salt or low-salt vegetable stock
4 tbsp passata
55 g/2 oz small pasta shapes
4 tbsp canned, no-salt, no-sugar haricot beans, drained and rinsed
25 g/1 oz spinach, washed and thick stalks removed, finely chopped
2 tbsp freshly grated Parmesan cheese

❹ Add the spinach and cook for a further 2 minutes, or until the spinach is tender. Stir in the Parmesan cheese and purée, mash or chop the mixture.

Spring Vegetable Risotto

PREPARATION TIME: 5 MINUTES	COOKING TIME: 35–40 MINUTES
FREEZING: SUITABLE	SERVES: 6–8 PORTIONS

Rice is perfect for babies as it is comforting and easy to eat. I have used spring vegetables here but do experiment.

❶ Steam the leek, courgette and peas for 5–8 minutes, until tender.

❷ Heat the oil and butter in a heavy-based saucepan. When the butter has melted, add the rice and stir for a couple of minutes until it is coated with the oil and has become translucent.

❸ Add the stock a ladleful at a time, waiting until it has been absorbed before adding more. Bring to the boil and simmer for 20 minutes, stirring continuously. Add the oregano, Parmesan and vegetables and simmer, stirring, for a further 5–10 minutes, until the liquid has been absorbed and the rice is tender. Purée the risotto for younger babies, adding extra stock or water if it is too thick.

INGREDIENTS:
1 small leek, peeled and finely chopped
1 small courgette, finely chopped
small handful of frozen peas
1 tsp olive oil
small knob of unsalted butter
85 g/3 oz arborio rice
350 ml/12 fl oz hot no-salt or low-salt vegetable or chicken stock
½ tsp dried oregano
2 tbsp freshly grated Parmesan cheese

Baked Plaice with Tomato Rice

PREPARATION TIME: 10 MINUTES	COOKING TIME: 30 MINUTES
FREEZING: SUITABLE	SERVES: 6–8 PORTIONS

The tomato rice can be served on its own if your baby is not ready for fish.

❶ Preheat the oven to 350°F/180°C/Gas Mark 4. Put the plaice on a large piece of baking paper, brush it with oil and arrange the fresh tomatoes on top. Fold up the baking paper to make a parcel and encase the fish. Place the parcel on a baking sheet and bake for 20 minutes.

❷ Put the rice and chopped tomatoes in a saucepan and cover with the water. Bring to the boil and add the basil, oregano, carrot and beans. Reduce the heat, cover, and simmer for 20 minutes, until the water has been absorbed and the rice, carrot and beans are tender.

❸ Remove the basil sprig. Remove the skin and any bones from the fish and flake the flesh. Fold the fish and fresh tomatoes into the tomato rice and serve puréed or mashed.

INGREDIENTS:
1 small plaice fillet
olive oil, for brushing
2 medium tomatoes, skinned, seeded and coarsely chopped
85 g/3 oz brown long-grain rice, washed
4 tbsp canned chopped tomatoes
175 ml/6 fl oz water
1 sprig of fresh basil leaves
½ tsp dried oregano
1 small carrot, peeled and diced
3 fine French beans, sliced

Chicken & Pineapple Cheese

PREPARATION TIME: 10 MINUTES	**COOKING TIME:** 15 MINUTES
FREEZING: UNSUITABLE	**SERVES:** 2 PORTIONS

This creamy dip couldn't be more simple or quick to make. Serve it mashed with fingers of toast or pitta bread, or blend to make a nutritious sandwich filling.

❶ Heat the oil in a non-stick frying pan. Add the chicken breast and cook for 12–15 minutes, turning occasionally, until tender and lightly browned. Set aside to cool slightly. Finely chop the chicken.

❷ Combine the chicken with the cottage cheese, yogurt and pineapple and mash together. Alternatively, place all the ingredients in a blender and blend the mixture to a coarse purée.

INGREDIENTS:

1 tsp olive oil
55 g/2 oz skinless chicken breast, chopped
4 tbsp cottage cheese
1 tbsp natural yogurt
1 slice of fresh pineapple, cored and diced

Pastina with Butternut Squash

PREPARATION TIME: 5 MINUTES	**COOKING TIME:** 15 MINUTES
FREEZING: SUITABLE	**SERVES:** 4–6 PORTIONS

This nurturing dish is a favourite weaning food in Italy.

❶ Steam the butternut squash for 10–15 minutes, until tender, and purée or mash with a fork.

❷ Meanwhile, cook the pasta according to the instructions on the packet, until it is tender. Add the butter, oil and Parmesan cheese and stir until the pasta is coated, then combine with the butternut squash.

INGREDIENTS:

85 g/3 oz butternut squash, peeled, seeded and chopped
85 g/3 oz baby pasta shapes or pastina
small knob of unsalted butter
1 tsp olive oil
2 tbsp freshly grated Parmesan cheese

Bean & Root Vegetable Mash

PREPARATION TIME: 5 MINUTES	COOKING TIME: 20 MINUTES
FREEZING: SUITABLE	SERVES: 4 PORTIONS

This comforting combination is a favourite with little ones and adults alike. For young babies, the beans should be mashed or puréed until smooth.

❶ Cook the potato and swede in boiling water for 15–20 minutes, until tender. Drain and purée or mash with the olive oil and butter.

❷ Heat the beans through and mash or chop, depending on the age of your baby. Peel the egg and discard the white. Mash the egg yolk and combine with the beans and mashed potato.

INGREDIENTS:
1 medium potato, peeled and cubed
85 g/3 oz swede or celeriac, peeled and cubed
1 tsp olive oil
small knob of unsalted butter or margarine
4 tbsp no-salt, no-sugar baked beans
1 hard-boiled egg yolk

Tuna Salad

PREPARATION TIME: 5 MINUTES
FREEZING: UNSUITABLE   SERVES: 4–6 PORTIONS

Babies from 8 months can enjoy this first introduction to salad. It works well as a dip with breadsticks, pitta bread and sticks of raw or steamed carrot, baby sweetcorn, red pepper, cucumber and apple, or spread over rice cakes or bread.

❶ Place the tuna, avocado, cottage cheese, yogurt, tomato, chives and lemon juice in a bowl and mash until combined and smooth or to the desired consistency.

INGREDIENTS:
2 tbsp canned tuna in oil, drained and mashed
½ avocado, peeled, stoned and chopped
4 tbsp cottage cheese
1 tbsp natural yogurt
1 medium tomato, skinned, seeded and finely chopped
1 tsp finely chopped fresh chives
squeeze of fresh lemon juice

Houmus with Crudités

PREPARATION TIME: 10 MINUTES	
FREEZING: UNSUITABLE	SERVES: 10 PORTIONS

Houmus not only makes a nutritious, convenient snack, but a spoonful stirred into a soup or sauce can also add substance and flavour. Choose from the selection of crudités mentioned below, but for young babies the vegetables should be steamed to make them easier to eat.

❶ Place the chickpeas in a blender with the garlic, tahini, lemon juice and yogurt. Blend until smooth.

❷ Store in the refrigerator for up to 3 days and serve with the crudités, which can be steamed or raw.

❸ The following fruits and vegetables can be used as crudités for this dip: slices of apple, pear and peach; sticks of carrot, French beans, red pepper, baby sweetcorn and mangetout.

INGREDIENTS:
200 g/7 oz no-salt, no-sugar canned chickpeas, drained and rinsed
½ clove garlic, crushed
3 tbsp tahini
freshly squeezed lemon juice, to taste
1 tbsp natural yogurt

Apricot Porridge

PREPARATION TIME: 10 MINUTES, PLUS OVERNIGHT SOAKING		
COOKING TIME: 15 MINUTES	FREEZING: SUITABLE	SERVES: 4 PORTIONS

Most of the following desserts can double up as a breakfast, which is worth remembering if you have plenty left over. The dried apricots are cooked and puréed and are delicious with yogurt or fromage frais. Dates make a good alternative.

❶ Wash and soak the apricots in cold water overnight. The next day, drain the apricots and place in a saucepan. Cover with water and bring to the boil, then reduce the heat and simmer for 10–15 minutes, until soft.

❷ Purée the cooked apricots in a blender until smooth, adding a little of the cooking water if necessary.

INGREDIENTS:
6 unsulphured dried, ready-to-eat apricots
8 tbsp porridge oats

❸ Meanwhile, cover the oats with half water and half milk. Bring to the boil, reduce the heat and simmer for 5–8 minutes, until the oats are tender. Combine with the apricot purée.

Banana Yogurt Custard

PREPARATION TIME: 5 MINUTES
FREEZING: UNSUITABLE SERVES: 2 PORTIONS

Bananas, when they are well-ripened, are easy for your baby to digest and can be mashed into a smooth paste. This pudding is a good way of introducing yogurt into your child's diet, and it is more exciting when blended with the banana and custard.

❶ Combine the mashed banana with the yogurt, custard and vanilla essence and mix well.

INGREDIENTS:
1 small banana, mashed
2 tbsp Greek-style yogurt
2 tbsp made-up custard
few drops of vanilla essence

Fromage Frais & Mango Purée

PREPARATION TIME: 5 MINUTES COOKING TIME: 2 MINUTES
FREEZING: UNSUITABLE SERVES: 2 PORTIONS

Any of the fruit purées mentioned earlier can replace the mango in this recipe. The wheatgerm is a good source of fibre, vitamins and minerals but it can be left out.

❶ Steam the mango for 2 minutes or, if very ripe, mash with a fork and pass through a sieve until smooth. Mix together well with the fromage frais and wheatgerm.

INGREDIENTS:
½ small ripe mango, peeled and chopped
4–6 tbsp fromage frais
1 tsp wheatgerm

Apple & Plum Yogurt

PREPARATION TIME: 5 MINUTES	COOKING TIME: 5 MINUTES
FREEZING: UNSUITABLE	SERVES: 2 PORTIONS

Babies can dislike the texture of plums, so mixing them with apple and yogurt can make them more baby friendly.

❶ Put the apple and plums into a saucepan with the water. Bring to the boil and cook for 5 minutes, until tender. Remove the plum skins and purée in a blender or pass through a sieve until smooth.

❷ Mix together the fruit purée and yogurt and sprinkle over the crushed biscuit before serving.

INGREDIENTS:
2 tbsp water
1 small dessert apple, peeled, cored and chopped
2 ripe plums, stoned
4–6 tbsp natural yogurt
1 plain biscuit, crushed

Sunset Jelly

PREPARATION TIME: 15 MINUTES PLUS SETTING
FREEZING: UNSUITABLE   SERVES: 4 PORTIONS

Cubes of jelly are interspersed with pieces of fruit in this vibrant pudding. The yogurt is a good source of calcium.

❶ Make the jelly as instructed on the packet, using the water. Whisk in the yogurt and allow to cool, then refrigerate until set.

❷ Cut the jelly into cubes, dipping the knife into warm water to prevent it sticking. Arrange in a bowl with the melon and peach.

INGREDIENTS:
½ pack of red jelly (raspberry, strawberry or cherry)
250 ml/8 fl oz boiling water
1 tbsp peach yogurt
1 slice of Galia melon, cubed
1 small ripe peach, peeled, stoned and cubed

NINE TO TWELVE MONTHS

This can be a challenging but rewarding stage in a baby's development. There will be fewer occasions when a specially prepared meal is required, and he or she may start to enjoy the social aspect of eating with the family. At this stage, babies will also begin to exercise their desire for independence and a growing curiosity for what's around them. This can prove an interesting time, and plenty of patience and a sense of humour are vital!

Eating with the Family

Health practitioners refer to this period as the third stage of weaning, when most babies are accustomed to chewing small pieces of food and are able to join in most family meals. Your baby will now be sitting in a high chair and will probably have a few teeth, but may also become more fussy about what he or she eats.

BELOW *It is a good feeling when your baby is able to join in with the family meal and enjoy it!*

New tastes

Although you still have to restrict your baby's food salt intake and avoid whole nuts, honey, soft or blue cheese, chillies, shellfish and raw eggs, almost anything else goes. You may find that your baby rejects particular foods but it's essential not to make an issue of this. Your baby is unlikely to love everything that is presented before him or her and teething and general well-being can influence likes and dislikes on an almost daily basis. Try to offer the food again at a later stage. The term 'balanced diet' can instil fear in most of us, but as long as your baby is eating a good mix of foods, including breads and cereals, lean meat, fish and poultry, dairy products, beans and lentils and plenty of fruit and vegetables, then you are providing a range of nutrients. As mentioned before, ensure your baby is eating sufficient amounts of iron-rich food (see page 7). Iron is essential for good health and a deficiency can lead to irritability, anaemia and a poor immune system.

Three meals a day

Babies seem to thrive on routine and because their stomachs are small they require three meals, plus a couple of snacks a day. The following menu also gives suggestions for light suppers but you may feel this is unnecessary. Ideally, and if convenient, the main meal of the day should be lunch. Babies seem to be more open to new tastes at this time of day, when they are alert and less fractious – the same can be said of parents! It also allows the digestive system to cope with unfamiliar new foods. At this stage baby foods don't need to be puréed. Coarsely mashed, grated and chopped foods will help your child's teeth and allow them to practise their chewing skills. Good hygiene practices are paramount but it is now unnecessary to sterilise every eating utensil that your baby uses. This is with the exception of bottles and teats, which are difficult to clean and can be a breeding ground for germs.

Milk and drinks

Milk remains an important source of nutrients and your baby still requires about 600 ml/1 pint a day, although some of this can be provided by milky puddings and sauces and in breakfast cereals. Avoid giving cow's milk as a drink, opting for breast, formula or follow-on milk instead. Offer water or unsweetened fruit juice, 1 part juice to 5 parts water, at mealtimes.

Finger foods

Finger foods can offer relief to teething babies. Lightly steamed sticks of vegetables or peeled raw fruit are ideal for helping sore gums, especially if they are chilled. Fingers of bread, slowly dried in the oven, are a healthy alternative to commercial baby rusks. Fingers of pitta, chapatti, muffins or naan bread can be dipped into houmus or vegetable purées, but make sure you never leave a baby unattended while eating because of possible choking.

MEAL PLANNER 3

9–12 MONTHS	BREAKFAST	MID-MORNING	LUNCH	TEA	SUPPER	BEDTIME
			(with diluted unsweetened fruit juice – 1 part juice: 5 parts water – or cooled boiled water)	(same drink as lunch)	(same drink as tea)	
Day 1	Coconut muesli Toast & milk	Milk	Herby vegetable & pasta cheese Banana cinnamon toast	Tuna salad New potatoes Fromage frais	Green fingers Tortilla/pitta bread Fruit	Milk
Day 2	Well-cooked scrambled egg Grilled tomatoes Toast & milk	Milk	Moroccan chicken couscous Baked apple crumblies	Muffin pizzas Houmus & crudités Banana yogurt custard	Pastina Vegetable fingers Fruit	Milk
Day 3	Weetabix & banana Muffin & milk	Milk	Baked plaice with tomato rice Sunny sundae	Bean & root vegetable mash Apple & plum yogurt	Sandwich Fruit	Milk
Day 4	Apricot porridge Milk & toast	Milk	Chinese rice with omelette strips Banana cinnamon toast	Pink pasta salad Baked potato Ice cream	Houmus & crudités Pitta bread Fruit	Milk
Day 5	Ready Brek Fruit bread Milk	Milk	Chicken & pineapple cheese Garlic bread Baked apple crumblies	Pastina Broccoli Fromage frais	Sandwich Fruit	Milk
Day 6	Coconut muesli Toast & milk	Milk	Mini meatballs in tomato sauce Sunny sundae	Minestrone soup Chocolate cinnamon rice pudding	Cheese on toast Fruit	Milk
Day 7	Well-cooked poached egg Toasted muffin & milk	Milk	Creamy salmon & broccoli pasta Sunset jelly	Spring vegetable risotto Banana & custard	Green fingers Tortilla/pitta bread Fruit	Milk

Chinese Rice with Omelette Strips

PREPARATION TIME: 10 MINUTES	COOKING TIME: 10 MINUTES
FREEZING: SUITABLE IF RICE NOT FROZEN BEFORE	SERVES: 2 PORTIONS

This is a great way of using up leftover cooked rice and surplus vegetables. Make sure you use cold rice and reheat it thoroughly before serving. Soy sauce is very salty, so just a splash should suffice in this dish.

❶ Heat the vegetable oil and sesame oil in a wok or heavy-based frying pan. Add the garlic, five spice, carrot and sweetcorn and stir-fry for 5 minutes, stirring and tossing continuously to prevent the spices and vegetables burning and sticking.

❷ Add the water and stir-fry for 2 minutes, then mix in the spinach and cook, stirring frequently, for a further 2 minutes, or until the vegetables are tender.

❸ Add the rice and a splash of soy sauce to the wok or pan and heat through thoroughly. Mix in the sesame seeds, if using.

❹ Meanwhile, melt the butter in a small heavy-based frying pan and add the egg. Swirl the egg until it covers the base of the pan. Cook

INGREDIENTS:
2 tsp vegetable oil
few drops of sesame oil
1 small clove garlic, finely chopped
pinch of Chinese five spice
1 carrot, peeled and diced
2 baby sweetcorn, halved and thinly sliced
2 tbsp water
small handful of baby spinach, tough stems removed and finely sliced
175 g/6 oz cold, cooked brown or white rice
dash of soy sauce
1 tsp sesame seeds, optional
small knob of unsalted butter
1 egg, beaten

until the egg has set and is cooked through, then turn out onto a plate. Cut the omelette into strips or pieces.

❺ Place the rice in a bowl and arrange the omelette in a criss-cross pattern on top.

Herby Vegetable & Pasta Cheese

PREPARATION TIME: 10 MINUTES	COOKING TIME: 15 MINUTES
FREEZING: SUITABLE	SERVES: 4–6 PORTIONS

Although I've used broccoli and cauliflower here, this creamy cheese sauce goes well with many vegetables.

❶ Steam the broccoli and cauliflower for 8–10 minutes, until tender. Cook the pasta according to the instructions on the packet, until the pasta is tender, then drain.

❷ Meanwhile, make the cheese sauce. Melt the butter in a small heavy-based saucepan over a low heat. Gradually add the flour, beating well to form a smooth paste. Cook for 30 seconds, stirring continuously. Add the milk, whisking well, then stir in the oregano. Simmer for 2 minutes until smooth and creamy, then mix in the cheese. Stir until melted.

INGREDIENTS:
4 florets broccoli, cut into small florets
4 florets cauliflower, cut into small florets
85 g/3 oz small penne or farfalle pasta
CHEESE SAUCE
1½ tbsp unsalted butter or margarine
1 tbsp plain flour
175 ml/6 fl oz full cream milk
½ tsp dried oregano
55 g/2 oz Cheddar cheese, grated

❸ Add the cooked cauliflower, broccoli and pasta to the cheese sauce and stir well. Finely chop or mash the mixture.

Creamy Salmon & Broccoli Pasta

PREPARATION TIME: 10 MINUTES	COOKING TIME: 15 MINUTES
FREEZING: UNSUITABLE	SERVES: 2–4 PORTIONS

This delicious combination of cream cheese, salmon and broccoli is a good introduction to the benefits of oily fish.

❶ Cook the pasta according to the instructions on the packet, until tender, then drain. Steam the broccoli for 8–10 minutes, until tender.

❷ At the same time, prepare the sauce. Heat the oil and butter in a small heavy-based frying pan, then add the leek and cook for 7 minutes, or until softened. Add the salmon and cook for 2 minutes, or until just cooked and opaque. Stir in the cream cheese and milk and heat through.

INGREDIENTS:
85 g/3 oz small pasta shells
55 g/2 oz broccoli florets
1 tsp oil
small knob of unsalted butter
1 small leek, finely chopped
140 g/5 oz salmon fillet, skin and bones removed, cubed
4 tbsp garlic and herb cream cheese
2–3 tbsp full cream milk

❸ Combine the sauce with the pasta and broccoli. Chop or mash the mixture finely as desired.

Moroccan Chicken Couscous

PREPARATION TIME: 10 MINUTES	COOKING TIME: 15 MINUTES
FREEZING: UNSUITABLE	SERVES: 4 PORTIONS

This recipe may sound exotic but it really is very easy to make and features just a hint of spice. Likes and dislikes develop at an early age so now is the time to encourage diverse tastes.

❶ Place the couscous in a bowl and pour over boiling water until just covered. Leave until all the water has been absorbed, for about 8–10 minutes, then mix in the butter and fluff up with a fork.

❷ Meanwhile, heat half the oil in a heavy-based frying pan and add the onion and sauté for about 7 minutes, until softened. Add the chicken, garlic, cumin and coriander and cook, stirring occasionally, for a further 5–8 minutes, until the chicken is cooked and tender.

INGREDIENTS:
55 g/2 oz couscous
small knob of unsalted butter
3 tsp olive oil
1 small onion, finely chopped
1 small skinless chicken breast, cut into bite-sized pieces
1 small clove garlic, finely chopped
½ tsp ground cumin
pinch of ground coriander
1 small peach or nectarine, stoned and diced
4 whole toasted almonds, finely chopped

❸ Carefully mix in the couscous, peach and almonds and heat through gently, stirring occasionally.

Mini Meatballs in Tomato Sauce

PREPARATION TIME: 10 MINUTES	COOKING TIME: 30 MINUTES
FREEZING: SUITABLE	SERVES: 2 PORTIONS

These succulent meatballs are very versatile and make good burgers. Here, they are cooked in a rich tomato sauce.

❶ To make the meatballs, place all the ingredients in a blender and process until combined and formed into a smooth mixture. Shape the mixture into small balls. Set them aside in the fridge.

❷ To make the tomato sauce, heat the oil in a small heavy-based frying pan. Add the onion and sauté for 7 minutes, until softened and translucent. Add the chopped tomatoes, bay leaf, tomato purée and oregano.

❸ Add the meatballs and simmer, half covered, for 20 minutes, or until the meatballs are cooked. Turn the meatballs occasionally during

INGREDIENTS:
meatballs:
12 g/½ oz fresh breadcrumbs
25 g/1 oz cup freshly grated Parmesan cheese, plus extra for the topping
140 g/5 oz good-quality mince
1 small egg, beaten
1 small clove garlic, crushed (optional)
tomato sauce:
1 tsp olive oil
1 small onion, finely chopped
300 ml/½ pint chopped tomatoes
1 bay leaf
1 tsp tomato purée
½ tsp dried oregano

cooking. Remove the bay leaf and sprinkle the balls with more Parmesan, if liked.

Muffin Pizzas

PREPARATION TIME: 10 MINUTES	COOKING TIME: 20 MINUTES
FREEZING: SUITABLE	SERVES: 2 PORTIONS

I've used muffins as a base for these simple pizzas but you could try focaccia, a wholemeal bap or pitta bread. Toppings can be equally varied: choose from tomato, mozzarella cheese, sweetcorn, pepper, salami or chopped olives.

❶ Preheat the oven to 200°C/400°F/Gas Mark 6. Heat the olive oil in a saucepan. Add the garlic and fry for 1 minute, until softened but not browned. Add the tomatoes and oregano. Cook over a low heat, stirring occasionally, for 5–8 minutes, or until reduced and thickened.

INGREDIENTS:
1 tsp olive oil
½ clove garlic, crushed
90 ml/3 fl oz chopped tomatoes
1 tsp dried oregano
1–2 wholemeal/white muffins, halved
20 g/¾ oz/z Cheddar cheese, grated
40 g/1½ oz mozzarella cheese, sliced

❷ Spoon a little tomato sauce over each muffin half, then sprinkle the Cheddar and mozzarella cheeses over the top.

❸ Place the muffins on a baking sheet and bake in the oven for 10 minutes, or until the topping is bubbling and golden.

Green Fingers

PREPARATION TIME: 10 MINUTES
FREEZING: SUITABLE   SERVES: 2 PORTIONS

Serve this creamy, garlicky guacamole dip with soft, floury tortillas and sticks of steamed or raw carrot, pepper, cucumber, baby sweetcorn and mangetout. A spoonful of guacamole makes a nutritious addition to soups and stews.

❶Put the avocado, garlic and lemon juice into a bowl. Mash with a fork until fairly smooth and creamy.

❷Warm the tortillas in a large dry frying pan. Spread the guacamole over the tortillas and cut into fingers or wedges, or roll them up.

INGREDIENTS:
2 soft tortillas
½ avocado, stoned and flesh scooped out
½ clove garlic, crushed
squeeze of fresh lemon juice

Pink Pasta Salad

PREPARATION TIME: 10 MINUTES	COOKING TIME: 10–15 MINUTES
FREEZING: UNSUITABLE	SERVES: 2–4 PORTIONS

Salad may not spring to mind as a suitable infant food but this one may change your ideas, and a novel-shaped pasta will add to its appeal. The choice of salad ingredients can also be varied according to your baby's likes and dislikes.

❶ Cook the pasta according to the instructions on the packet, until the pasta is tender. Drain and set aside.

❷ Steam the pepper for 2 minutes, until softened.

❸ Place the pasta, pepper, tomatoes, sweetcorn and ham, if using, in a bowl. Mix together the pesto and mayonnaise and spoon the mixture over the salad ingredients. Mix everything together well to coat all the ingredients in the sauce.

INGREDIENTS:
85 g/3 oz fun-shaped pasta
½ small red pepper, seeded and diced
2 tomatoes, seeded and diced
2 tbsp canned sweetcorn, drained and rinsed
1–2 slices of ham or 1 cooked sausage, diced (optional)
2 tbsp red pesto
1–2 tbsp mayonnaise

Coconut Muesli

PREPARATION TIME: 10 MINUTES	
FREEZING: UNSUITABLE	SERVES: 10 PORTIONS

This healthy breakfast of oats, nuts and dried fruit can double up as a nutritious pudding. For babies up to 12 months, serve the oaty cereal with breast or formula milk, allowing it to soften first in the milk before serving. Alternatively, soak the muesli in a little apple juice or water to soften the oats and stir a spoonful into natural yogurt.

❶ Mix together the oats, wheat flakes, raisins, apricots, hazelnuts and coconut. Store the mixture in an airtight container.

❷ Just before serving, mix a few spoonfuls of the muesli with 2 tablespoons of freshly grated apple, if liked, or serve on its own.

INGREDIENTS:
115 g/4 oz porridge oats
115 g/4 oz wheat flakes
3 tbsp raisins
55 g/2 oz dried unsulphured apricots, finely chopped
55 g/2 oz roasted hazelnuts, finely chopped
25 g/1 oz desiccated coconut
freshly grated apple (optional)

Sunny Sundae

PREPARATION TIME: 10 MINUTES	**COOKING TIME:** 3 MINUTES
FREEZING: UNSUITABLE	**SERVES:** 2–4 PORTIONS

Named after the vibrant colour of the mango and orange purée, this pretty pudding is also good served with thick natural yogurt instead of the ice cream.

❶ Put three-quarters of the orange and mango in a small heavy-based saucepan and add the maple syrup and water. Bring to the boil, then reduce the heat and simmer for 2 minutes, or until the fruit has softened. You may need to add a little extra water if the fruit seems too dry.

❷ Transfer the fruit to a blender and purée until smooth. Press the fruit through a sieve to remove any fibres or membranes, if necessary.

❸ Place the reserved fruit in a serving bowl and top with a scoop of ice cream. Spoon over the orange and mango purée and sprinkle with the crushed biscuits. Yogurt can be used in the place of ice cream.

INGREDIENTS:

1 orange, peeled and segmented

1 small mango, peeled, stoned and chopped

1–2 tbsp maple syrup, according to taste

1 tbsp water

2–4 scoops vanilla ice cream

1–2 digestive biscuits, crushed

Banana Cinnamon Toast

PREPARATION TIME: 5 MINUTES	**COOKING TIME:** 3 MINUTES
FREEZING: UNSUITABLE	**SERVES:** 1 PORTION

A melt-in-the-mouth pudding or breakfast, which is popular with children and adults alike. Wholemeal toast, pannetone or fruit bread are just as delicious as the muffins used here.

❶ Melt the butter in a small heavy-based frying pan. Add the banana pieces and cook for 1 minute, turning to coat them in the butter.

❷ Add the maple syrup and cinnamon and cook the banana for 1–2 minutes, until softened. Gently stir in the toasted almonds, if using.

❸ Cut the toasted fruit muffin into fingers or wedges and spoon over the cooked banana. Serve with the Greek-style yogurt, either as a topping or on the side.

INGREDIENTS:

1 tbsp unsalted butter

1 small banana, peeled and sliced diagonally

2 tbsp maple syrup

¼ tsp ground cinnamon

sprinkling of chopped toasted almonds, to serve (optional)

½ fruit muffin, toasted

1 tbsp Greek-style yogurt, to serve

Baked Apple Crumblies

PREPARATION TIME: 10 MINUTES **COOKING TIME:** 45 MINUTES

FREEZING: UNSUITABLE **SERVES:** 4–8 PORTIONS

This variation on the classic apple crumble uses whole apples, which are filled with dried fruit and topped with an oaty crumble. Serve the apples with custard, cream or ice cream.

❶ Preheat the oven to 180°C/350°F/ Gas Mark 4. Core each apple and score the skin around the middle to stop the apples bursting.

❷ Put the flour and butter in a bowl and, using your fingertips, rub into coarse breadcrumbs. Add the oats and sugar and mix well. Combine the dates and raisins in a separate bowl.

❸ Half fill the cavity of each apple with the dried fruit, then top with the crumble mixture.

INGREDIENTS:
4 small cooking apples, such as Bramley
40 g/1½ oz plain flour, sifted
2 tbsp unsalted butter, cubed
2 tbsp porridge oats
3 tbsp soft light brown sugar
55 g/2 oz dried, ready-to-eat dates, stoned and finely chopped
25 g/1 oz raisins

❹ Place the apples in an oven-proof dish and pour in a little water. Bake for 45 minutes, until the apples are tender.

Chocolate Cinnamon Rice Pudding

PREPARATION TIME: 5 MINUTES **COOKING TIME:** 2 HOURS

FREEZING: SUITABLE **SERVES:** 4 PORTIONS

Yummy! The ultimate comfort food, this rice pudding is even more delicious topped with sliced bananas or finely chopped roasted almonds or hazelnuts.

❶ Preheat the oven to 150°C/325°F/Gas Mark 3. Warm the milk and cocoa powder in a saucepan over a low heat. Whisk until the cocoa blends into the milk, then remove from the heat.

INGREDIENTS:
600 ml/1 pint full cream milk
3 tsp good quality cocoa powder
70 g/2½ oz pudding rice
3 tsp caster sugar
½ tsp ground cinnamon

❷ Place the rice in a small ovenproof dish, then pour in the chocolate milk. Sprinkle with the sugar and cinnamon and stir everything together well.

❸ Cover the dish and bake in the oven for 2 hours, or until most of the milk has been absorbed and the rice is very tender. Leave to cool slightly before serving.

TWELVE TO EIGHTEEN MONTHS

From around their first birthday, you should find that toddlers prefer to exercise their own independence – and mealtimes are the perfect opportunity! This can be a rewarding but also a frustrating time. Don't worry or make a fuss if your toddler refuses to eat. They all go through periods of faddy eating, and coaxing and encouragement are undoubtedly far more successful than force feeding. This approach also means peaceful mealtimes.

Eating on their own

Toddlers inevitably turn their noses up at some foods presented to them, but the best way to deal with fads and picky eating is to ignore them, however difficult and frustrating this may be. Habits are formed early, so stick to your guns and try to encourage your toddler to experience a variety of foods – encompassing a range of flavours, colours and textures – so they get used to trying new things.

ABOVE *Making mealtimes fun and less threatening can result in a less fussy child who is willing to try new foods.*

Healthy choice

Many of us have the preconceived idea that toddlers prefer bland, mushy foods, and consequently resort to so-called 'children's food'. Researchers at the University of Birmingham, however, have discovered that toddlers are far more open to new tastes and stronger flavours than previously thought. The popularity of garlic bread, houmus and garlic butter is testimony to this.

While it is not always feasible for the family to eat together, you will reap the benefits even if you only manage communal mealtimes at weekends. Although the target is to encourage your toddler to eat the same foods as the rest of the family, a high-fibre, low-fat diet is unsuitable for young children. Instead provide a good balance of high-energy, nutrient-dense foods, including plenty of fruit and vegetables, full-fat dairy produce, carbohydrates in the form of breads, pasta, potatoes and rice, as well as protein foods, including lean meat, poultry, fish, beans, eggs and different vegetarian alternatives.

Fussy Eating

If your toddler happily eats everything that is presented to him or her, then you really are extremely lucky and are likely to be in the minority. Toddlers of this age are too busy or distracted to sit down and eat. A simple way around this is to give your child his or her own spoon and bowl containing a little food, which can be topped up if necessary. (Smaller portions are less off-putting.) Finger foods are also popular and will allow your toddler his or her desired independence.

Toddlers can be incredibly fickle, loving a certain food one day and disliking it the next, and their appetite can be equally unpredictable.

Imaginative presentation can also make the difference. This doesn't mean spending hours creating complicated pictures out of every meal, but do try to choose different coloured and textured foods and arrange them in an attractive pattern. Brightly coloured plates can also help to make eating fun.

Milk and drinks

Cow's milk can be given as a drink at this stage, as well as used in cooking. While you may still be breastfeeding, it is no longer necessary to provide formula or follow-on milk, but this does mean that you should take care to ensure that your toddler's diet contains the required vitamins, minerals, fat, protein and carbohydrates.

Recipes

The recipes in this chapter have been created to appeal to toddlers and adults alike with the odd concession to healthy versions of so-called 'children's food'. I've tried to include a wide collection of dishes incorporating a range of flavours and textures. If time allows, encourage your toddler to get involved in the preparation of meals – it can be a fun time for the whole family.

MEAL PLANNER 4

12–18 MONTHS	BREAKFAST	LUNCH	TEA	SUPPER	BEDTIME
		(with diluted unsweetened fruit juice – 1 part juice: 5 parts water – or cooled boiled water)	(same drink as lunch)	(same drink as tea)	
Day 1	Granola, toast, milk	Vegetable & chickpea coconut curry & rice Quick summer pudding	Quick tuna pasta & broccoli Sunny sundae	Banana cinnamon toast Fruit	Milk
Day 2	Boiled egg Soldiers with yeast extract, yogurt, milk	Cottage pie & French beans Apple sponge pudding	Minestrone soup Garlic bread Strawberry yogurt lolly	Muffin pizza Fruit	Milk
Day 3	Coconut muesli Muffin, milk	Oodles of noodles Fromage frais & mango	Baked plaice with tomato rice, vegetables Apple & coconut cookies	Scrambled egg on toast Fruit	Milk
Day 4	Weetabix & banana Toast, milk	Gammon & pineapple rice, broccoli Baked apple crumblies	Creamy tomato soup Wholemeal bread Yogurt	Green fingers Pitta bread Grated cheese, fruit	Milk
Day 5	Poached egg & beans Soda bread, milk	Two-fish pasta bake, vegetables Chocolate cinnamon rice pudding	Pink pasta salad Breadsticks Apple & coconut cookies	Sandwich Fruit	Milk
Day 6	Porridge, toast, milk	Moroccan chicken couscous Vegetables Sunset jelly	Creamy salmon & broccoli pasta Strawberry yogurt lolly	Cheese on toast Fruit	Milk
Day 7	Scotch pancakes & fruit Yogurt, milk	Mini meatballs in tomato sauce Rice & vegetables Sunny sundae	Pesto potatoes Grated carrot Banana yogurt custard	Houmus, vegetable sticks, tortilla Fruit	Milk

Vegetable & Chickpea Coconut Curry

PREPARATION TIME: 10 MINUTES	COOKING TIME: 30 MINUTES
FREEZING: SUITABLE	SERVES: 4–6 PORTIONS

I've found this mild and creamy curry goes down well with older babies. For adults, bump up the quantity of spices.

❶ Cook the potatoes in boiling water for 10 minutes, or until tender. Add the cauliflower to the potatoes 5 minutes before the end of the cooking time.

❷ Meanwhile, heat the oil in a heavy-based saucepan, add the garlic and sauté for 1 minute, until softened but not coloured. Mix in the spices and cook.

❸ Put the vegetable stock and creamed coconut into a jug and stir until the coconut has dissolved. Add the stock mixture to the pan with the fresh tomatoes and tomato purée. Cook for 15 minutes, stirring occasionally, until thickened.

INGREDIENTS:
3 new potatoes, peeled and quartered
8 small cauliflower florets
2 tsp vegetable oil
1 small clove garlic, chopped
1 tsp garam masala
½ tsp turmeric
200 ml/7 fl oz hot vegetable stock
35 g/1¼ oz creamed coconut, chopped into small pieces
2 tomatoes, seeded and chopped
1 tbsp tomato purée
small handful of spinach leaves, tough stalks removed and finely shredded
4 tbsp canned chickpeas, drained and rinsed

❹ Add the spinach and chickpeas to the pan and cook for 2 minutes, until tender. Add the potatoes and cauliflower and mash or chop.

Two-Fish Pasta Bake

PREPARATION TIME: 10 MINUTES	COOKING TIME: 45 MINUTES
FREEZING: SUITABLE	SERVES: 4–6 PORTIONS

This fish pie is topped with pasta and mozzarella cheese rather than mashed potato.

❶ Preheat the oven to 200°C/400°F/Gas Mark 6. Cook the pasta according to the instructions on the packet until tender. Drain well. Toss in oil.

❷ Bring a small saucepan of water to the boil and add the egg. Cook for 8–10 minutes, until the egg is hard boiled. Cool the egg under cold running water.

❸ Heat the oil in a heavy-based frying pan. Add the onion and sauté for 5 minutes, until softened, then add the celery and carrot and sauté for 3 minutes. Add the spinach and cook for a further 2 minutes, until it is tender.

❹ Stir in the milk and cream and bring to the boil. Turn off the heat and stir in the Cheddar cheese, mustard, parsley and lemon juice.

INGREDIENTS:
85 g/3 oz penne or macaroni
2 tsp olive oil, plus extra for coating pasta
1 egg
1 small onion, finely chopped
1 small celery stick, finely chopped
1 small carrot, peeled and finely chopped
small handful of spinach leaves, tough stalks removed and finely shredded
120 ml/4 fl oz full cream milk
2 tbsp double cream
25 g/1 oz mature Cheddar cheese, grated
½ tsp English mustard
1 tbsp finely chopped fresh parsley
squeeze of fresh lemon juice
90 g/3¼ oz undyed smoked haddock, skin and bones removed
140 g/5 oz cod fillet, skin and bones removed
85 g/3 oz mozzarella cheese, broken into small pieces

❺ Place the fish in an ovenproof dish. Arrange the eggs, sauce, pasta and cheese on top. Bake for 20–25 minutes, until brown on top.

Oodles of Noodles

PREPARATION TIME: 10 MINUTES	**COOKING TIME:** 15 MINUTES
FREEZING: UNSUITABLE	**SERVES:** 4–6 PORTIONS

Noodles are both fun and versatile, so it's no surprise that they're loved by children. Take care when introducing peanuts as more people are becoming allergic to them.

❶ Steam the broccoli for 8 minutes, or until just tender. Meanwhile, cook the noodles according to the instructions on the packet, until tender, then drain and cool under cold running water.

❷ At the same time, heat the oil in a wok or heavy-based frying pan. Add the garlic, ginger and coriander and sauté for 1 minute, stirring continuously. Add the chicken and French beans and stir-fry for a further 5–8 minutes, until the chicken is cooked.

❸ Mix together the coconut, water and peanut butter until combined, then pour the mixture over the chicken. Cook for 3 minutes, or until reduced and thickened.

❹ Add the noodles, broccoli, lemon juice, sweetcorn and soy sauce and heat through, stirring continuously. Chop to the desired consistency.

INGREDIENTS:
8 broccoli florets, cut into small florets
85 g/3 oz medium egg noodles
2 tsp vegetable oil
1 small clove garlic, chopped
1 tsp grated fresh root ginger
¼ tsp ground coriander
1 skinless chicken breast, cut into strips
4 fine French beans, finely sliced
15 g/½ oz creamed coconut, cut into small pieces
50 ml/2 fl oz hot water
2 heaped tbsp smooth peanut butter
squeeze of fresh lemon juice
55 g/2 oz canned sweetcorn, drained and rinsed
2 tsp soy sauce

VARIATION Replace the chicken with a handful of cooked prawns, adding them with the noodles in step 4. The beans can be replaced with peas.

Gammon & Pineapple Rice

| PREPARATION TIME: 10 MINUTES | COOKING TIME: 20 MINUTES |
| FREEZING: UNSUITABLE | SERVES: 2 PORTIONS |

A classic combination of ham and pineapple is presented in this baby-friendly dish.

❶ Place the rice in a saucepan. Cover with the water and bring to the boil. Reduce the heat, cover, and simmer for 15 minutes, until the water has been absorbed and the rice is cooked.

❷ Meanwhile, heat the grill to high. Brush the gammon with honey and grill for 8–10 minutes on each side, until cooked through. Cut the meat into bite-sized pieces.

❸ At the same time, melt the butter in a small heavy-based

| INGREDIENTS: |
| 55 g/2 oz long-grain rice, rinsed |
| 250 ml/8 fl oz water |
| 1 thick gammon steak |
| runny honey, for glazing |
| 2 tbsp unsalted butter |
| 3 tbsp sweetcorn, drained and rinsed |
| 85 g/3 oz fresh pineapple, cubed |
| 1 tbsp finely chopped fresh parsley |

saucepan and add the sweetcorn and pineapple and heat through for a minute or so. Add the rice, gammon and parsley to the pan and stir well to combine.

Cottage Pie

| PREPARATION TIME: 10 MINUTES | COOKING TIME: 45 MINUTES |
| FREEZING: SUITABLE | SERVES: 4–6 PORTIONS |

This is always a favourite and can be made with meat or vegetarian alternatives, such as soya or Quorn mince.

❶ Preheat the oven to 180°C/350°F/Gas Mark 4. Heat the oil in a heavy-based saucepan. Add the onion and garlic and sauté for 5 minutes until softened. Add the courgette, carrot, mushrooms and herbs and cook for a further 5 minutes. Add the mince and cook until browned.

❷ Add the cannellini beans, stock, chopped tomatoes and tomato purée to the mince and bring to the boil, then reduce the heat and simmer, half covered, for 10–15 minutes, until the sauce has thickened and reduced.

❸ Meanwhile, cook the potatoes in boiling water for 15 minutes, or until tender. Drain and mash.

❹ Put the mince mixture into an ovenproof casserole dish and spoon the mash over the top. Top with grated cheese. Bake in the oven for 20 minutes, until golden brown.

| INGREDIENTS: |
| 2 tsp olive oil |
| 1 small onion, finely chopped |
| 1 small clove garlic, finely chopped |
| 1 courgette, diced |
| 1 carrot, peeled and diced |
| 3 mushrooms, peeled and finely chopped |
| ½ tsp oregano |
| ½ tsp thyme |
| 1 bay leaf |
| 115 g/4 oz lean mince, soya or Quorn mince |
| 3 tbsp canned cannellini beans, drained and rinsed |
| 150 ml/¼ pint vegetable stock |
| 150 ml/¼ pint chopped tomatoes |
| 1 tbsp tomato purée |
| 2 potatoes, peeled and cubed |
| 1 heaped tbsp unsalted butter |
| 2–3 tbsp full cream milk |
| 25 g/1 oz Cheddar cheese, grated |

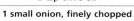

Creamy Tomato Soup with Garlic Croutons

PREPARATION TIME: 10 MINUTES   COOKING TIME: 45 MINUTES

FREEZING: SUITABLE   SERVES: 6 PORTIONS

Remarkably, children who turn their noses up at vegetables will happily eat them in this liquidised form.

❶ Preheat the oven to 200°C/400°F/Gas Mark 6. To make the garlic croutons, rub both sides of each slice of bread with the garlic. Cut the bread into cubes and put them into a small plastic bag with 2 tbsp olive oil. Shake the bag to coat the bread in the oil. Place the bread cubes on a baking sheet and bake for 10–12 minutes, until crisp and golden – keep an eye on the croutons as they burn easily.

❷ To make the soup, heat the remaining oil in a heavy-based saucepan. Add the onion, cover the pan, and sweat for 10 minutes, until softened. Add the carrot and potato and sweat for a further 2 minutes, stirring occasionally to prevent the vegetables sticking.

INGREDIENTS:
3 slices white bread or French stick, crusts removed
2 cloves garlic, peeled and halved
3 tbsp olive oil
1 tbsp olive oil
1 onion, chopped
1 carrot, peeled and finely chopped
1 small potato, peeled and cubed
500-g/1¼-lb carton creamed tomatoes
400 ml/14 fl oz vegetable stock

❸ Add the creamed tomatoes and stock and bring to the boil. Reduce the heat and simmer, half covered, for 25 minutes, until the vegetables are tender and the liquid has reduced and thickened.

❹ Carefully pour the mixture into a blender (or use a hand-held one) and process until smooth and creamy. Return the soup to the pan and heat through if necessary. Sprinkle with croutons before serving.

Quick Tuna Pasta

PREPARATION TIME: 5 MINUTES   COOKING TIME: 15 MINUTES

FREEZING: SUITABLE   SERVES: 2 PORTIONS

Tinned tuna and dried pasta are great storecupboard standbys and lend themselves to a multitude of dishes. The sugar helps to reduce the acidity of the tomatoes but it can be omitted if preferred.

❶ Cook the pasta according to the instructions on the packet until tender, then drain well.

❷ Meanwhile, heat the oil in a heavy-based saucepan. Add the garlic and sauté for 1 minute, until softened, stirring to prevent it sticking to the pan and burning. Pour in the wine, if using, and boil for a minute to evaporate it.

❸ Reduce the heat to medium, add the passata, sugar, basil and tuna to the pan and cook for a further 8–10 minutes, until the sauce has thickened and reduced. Stir in the

INGREDIENTS:
85 g/3 oz pasta shapes
2 tsp olive oil
1 small clove garlic, finely chopped
3 tbsp white wine (optional)
175 ml/6 fl oz passata
pinch of sugar (optional)
sprig of fresh basil
small tin tuna fish in oil, drained
1 tbsp fromage frais or houmus

fromage frais and warm over a low heat for a minute or so. Remove the sprig of basil and spoon the sauce over the pasta or mix the two together well. You can sprinkle cheese on top, if liked.

Pesto Potatoes

PREPARATION TIME: 15 MINUTES	**COOKING TIME:** 1–1½ HOURS
FREEZING: UNSUITABLE	**SERVES:** 1 PORTION

Baked potatoes have a lot going for them as they are easy to prepare, are filling and provide fibre, vitamins and minerals. I've included a recipe for pesto here but you could use a ready-made one if preferred. You can store it in an airtight jar in the refrigerator for up to a week.

❶ Preheat the oven to 200°C/ 400°F/Gas Mark 6. Bake the potato for 1–1½ hours, until it is tender.

❷ To make the pesto, place the basil, garlic and pine kernels in a blender and process until finely chopped. Gradually add the olive oil and then the Parmesan cheese and blend to a coarse purée.

❸ Steam the spinach for 3 minutes, or until tender. Squeeze out any excess water and chop.

❹ Cut the potato in half and scoop out most of the flesh, reserving the skins. Put the potato flesh in a bowl with 2 tablespoons of pesto and the spinach and mash until combined. Spoon the pesto mixture back into the potato skins and sprinkle with the Cheddar cheese.

INGREDIENTS:
1 small baking potato, scrubbed
handful of spinach leaves, shredded
1 tbsp freshly grated Cheddar or Parmesan cheese
PESTO
25 g/1 oz fresh basil leaves
1 clove garlic, crushed
15 g/¾ oz pine kernels
4 tbsp olive oil
2 tbsp freshly grated Parmesan cheese

❺ Place the potatoes under a hot grill for a minute or two until the cheese is bubbling and golden.

Granola

PREPARATION TIME: 5 MINUTES	**COOKING TIME:** 55 MINUTES
FREEZING: UNSUITABLE	**SERVES:** 10 PORTIONS

This honey-coated crunchy cereal contains none of the additives or large amounts of sugar that are found in many commercial alternatives but does contain fresh fruit, nuts and seeds. A spoonful can also be mixed into natural yogurt.

❶ Preheat the oven to 140°C/ 275°F/Gas Mark 1. Mix the oats, seeds and nuts together in a bowl.

❷ Heat the oil and honey in a saucepan until melted, then remove from the heat, add the oat mixture and stir well. Place the honey-coated oat mixture on two baking sheets in one layer.

❸ Cook for 40 minutes, or until crisp, stirring occasionally to prevent the mixture sticking to the baking

INGREDIENTS:
115 g/4 oz porridge oats
25 g/1 oz sunflower seeds
25 g/1 oz sesame seeds
50 g/2 oz roasted hazelnuts, finely chopped
2 tbsp sunflower oil
3 tbsp runny honey
50 g/2 oz raisins
50 g/2 oz dried, ready-to-eat apples, finely chopped

sheets. Remove from the oven and mix in the raisins and dried apple. Cool and store in a container.

Apple Sponge Pudding

PREPARATION TIME: 15 MINUTES	**COOKING TIME:** 40 MINUTES
FREEZING: UNSUITABLE	**SERVES:** 6 PORTIONS

This combination of tender cooked apples and vanilla sponge topping is delicious served cold with a scoop of ice cream.

❶ Preheat the oven to 180°C/350°F/ Gas Mark 4. Place the apples, 2 tablespoons of the sugar and the water in a heavy-based saucepan. Cover and cook over a low heat for 4–5 minutes, until the apples have softened. Stir in the cinnamon and transfer to an ovenproof dish.

❷ To make the sponge, beat the margarine with the remaining sugar using a wooden spoon, or process in a blender until light and creamy. Add the eggs, vanilla essence and flour. Beat or process the mixture to a soft, creamy consistency.

INGREDIENTS:
650 g/1 lb 7oz cooking apples, peeled, cored and sliced
100 g/3½ oz caster sugar
2 tbsp water
½ tsp ground cinnamon
6 tbsp margarine, softened
2 eggs, beaten
½ tsp vanilla essence
85 g/3 oz self-raising flour, sifted

❸ Spoon the sponge mixture over the apples and smooth it down gently with the back of a spoon. Bake for 30–35 minutes, until the sponge is risen and golden and springy to the touch.

Quick Summer Pudding

PREPARATION TIME: 15 MINUTES	**COOKING TIME:** 5 MINUTES
FREEZING: SUITABLE	**SERVES:** 2–4 PORTIONS

The classic summer pudding should be left overnight but this version tastes just as good and takes a fraction of the time to prepare. I've used pastry cutters to form the bread into fun shapes, but make sure they are the same size as the bread slices as small shapes will end up as a soggy, fruit-soaked mass.

❶ Put the berries in a saucepan with the sugar and water. Bring to the boil, then reduce the heat and simmer for 5 minutes, or until the fruit is soft and juicy.

❷ Cut the bread into your chosen shape(s) – make sure you have 2 of each shape – using a large pastry cutter. (The cutter should use as much of the bread slice as possible to avoid wastage.)

❸ Place half the bread shapes in a shallow dish, then spoon over the warm fruit. Place the remaining

INGREDIENTS:
450 g/1 lb mixed berries, such as strawberries, raspberries, blackcurrants or blackberries, hulled and the large fruit sliced
4–6 slices day-old white bread, crusts removed
4–5 tbsp caster sugar, according to taste
5 tbsp water
pastry cutters, such as hearts, stars or gingerbread people

bread shapes on top of the fruit and bread, then spoon over the warm juice. Press down lightly to soak the syrup into the bread. Leave for about 30 minutes before serving.

Strawberry Yogurt Lollies

PREPARATION TIME: 5 MINUTES	
FREEZING: SUITABLE	SERVES: 6

I've chosen strawberries because they are universally popular with children, but other types of fruit also go down well. The lollies are basically a frozen fruit smoothie, so they can be served in their unfrozen form too.

❶ Put the strawberries, yogurt, honey and vanilla essence in a blender and process until puréed.

❷ Pour the mixture into ice lolly moulds and freeze until solid. (Fun-shaped moulds are popular.)

INGREDIENTS:
350 g/12 oz fresh strawberries, hulled and sliced
300 g/10½ oz thick natural yogurt
3 tbsp honey
few drops of vanilla essence

TIP Most types of soft fruit can be used to make frozen lollies. Try raspberries, mango, peaches, nectarines, plums or melon, or try a combination.

Apple & Coconut Cookies

PREPARATION TIME: 15 MINUTES	COOKING TIME: 20 MINUTES
FREEZING: UNSUITABLE	SERVES: 12

These wholesome cookies have a soft, chewy texture, rather like flapjacks. Store in an airtight jar.

❶ Preheat the oven to 180°C/350°F/Gas Mark 4. Lightly grease 2 large baking sheets. Put the butter, sugar and syrup in a small saucepan. Cook over a gentle heat, until the butter melts and the sugar dissolves, stirring occasionally. Remove the pan from the heat.

❷ Put the grated apple, flour, coconut and oats in a large bowl, then add the syrup mixture. Mix with a wooden spoon to form a sticky dough. Place large spoonfuls of the mixture on the prepared baking sheets to make 12 cookies. Form the mixture into rounds, about 5 cm/2 in in diameter, leaving

INGREDIENTS:
115 g/4 oz unsalted butter, plus extra for greasing
85 g/3 oz caster sugar
2 tbsp golden syrup
2 eating apples, cored and grated
115 g/4 oz wholemeal self-raising flour
3 tbsp desiccated coconut
115 g/4 oz porridge oats

plenty of space around each one to allow them to spread.

❸ Bake for 15 minutes, or until golden and slightly crisp. Leave to cool slightly on the baking sheets, then transfer the cookies to a wire rack to cool.

EIGHTEEN TO THIRTY-SIX MONTHS

There is a world of difference between an 18-month and 3-year-old child, in terms of both behaviour and development. Yet similarities do exist – toddlers of both ages have a strong desire for independence, preferring to feed themselves, and can be fussy eaters at times. The following ideas will make mealtimes easier.

Good Eating Habits

As we have already learned, many nutritionists believe that good eating habits are formed in early childhood, so it is essential to encourage your toddler to try (and enjoy) a variety of foods, encompassing a range of flavours, colours and textures, when he or she is as young as possible. However, it's never too late to make healthy changes to your toddler's diet.

ABOVE *If you eat plenty of fresh fruit, your children should follow by example and accept this as normal.*

Fresh is best

In an ideal world, only home-cooked foods would pass our little ones' lips, yet this is unrealistic for most us. The biggest influence on our children's health is the quality and variety of ingredients used and, perhaps reassuringly, not all prepared foods are bad. The foods you should avoid are those where saturated or hydrogenated fats, colourings, additives, sweeteners, sugar and salt appear high in the ingredients list. Try to get into the habit of reading the list of ingredients and the nutritional information on the packet before you buy it. Having said this, a toddler's diet shouldn't rely on processed foods, and it is crucial to introduce freshly prepared meals at as young an age as possible. Habits are formed early and it's easier to avoid junk foods while children are small. Toddlers will inevitably turn their noses up at some foods, but the more choice they are given, the better — both for them and for you. Fresh foods don't have to take long to prepare, usually taste better than junk foods, and are more nutritious. If this wasn't enough to convince you, they're usually cheaper: with convenience foods you are actually paying for someone else to do the work for you!

Eating together

There are numerous reasons why it is not always possible for the family to eat together. However, you'll reap the benefits in the long term, even if you manage communal mealtimes only at the weekend. For the rest of the week, try at least to sit down with your toddler while he or she is eating, and perhaps have your own small portion of food. Toddlers learn by example and it also makes mealtimes a more enjoyable and social affair. Incidentally, try to ignore poor eating habits and you'll probably find your toddler will soon get bored with playing up. Instead, offer heaps of praise and encouragement when your toddler eats well.

Snack time

While some toddlers refuse to eat a complete meal, most relish snacks, especially if they can feed themselves. Take advantage of this by offering healthy snacks — this may be a way of supplementing an otherwise restricted diet. The following ideas may help when you are faced with a hungry toddler:

- Wedges of raw fruit and vegetables
- Breadsticks with houmus
- Fruit scones
- Rice cakes with low-salt yeast extract
- Slices of pitta bread with smooth peanut butter
- Fruit muffins with banana
- Natural yogurt with honey
- Fingers of pineapple with cream cheese
- Homemade vegetable crisps
- Carrot cake
- Low-salt tortilla chips, covered with grated cheese and grilled
- Oatcakes with pâté

What Does My Toddler Need?

Children over a year old can join in family meals, but their requirement for high-energy foods is still much greater than that of adults. Compared with the very rapid growth rate during the first year, your toddler is now growing more slowly. However, you'll find that he or she is far more active – walking, jumping and running – which means that extra calories and a varied, nutritious diet are essential for growth and proper development.

The term 'balanced diet' can intimidate even the most nutritionally aware parent. Yet as long as your toddler is eating a good mix of foods, including bread, pasta, rice, potatoes, fruits and vegetables, dairy foods, meat, fish and eggs, preferably on a daily or, if not, on a weekly basis, then that should be more than sufficient. Obviously this range of foods can vary depending on

RIGHT Offer raw vegetables and fruit as a snack instead of biscuits or cake.

BELOW LEFT Milk still forms an important part of a toddler's diet: cow's milk is fine.

special diets, eating preferences and the presence of any food intolerances or allergies. Choose foods from the food groups below and your toddler will almost certainly be getting all the nutrients he or she needs.

Starchy foods

Starchy foods, otherwise known as carbohydrates, include breakfast cereals, bread, pasta, rice and potatoes. These should form a major part of your toddler's diet as they are a good source of energy, fibre, vitamins and minerals. Wholegrain varieties, such as wholemeal bread, brown rice and pasta, provide the richest source of nutrients and fibre, yet should not be given in large amounts to young children. Unlike adults, toddlers find it difficult to digest large amounts of high-fibre foods, leading to stomach upsets and a reduced appetite. Fibre can also interfere with the absorption of certain minerals.

Fruits and vegetables

Fresh and frozen fruits and vegetables, more so than canned, are an essential part of a toddler's diet, providing rich amounts of vitamins, minerals and fibre. As with younger children, offer around four to five different types of fresh produce a day, such as citrus fruit, salad, and orange, red and green vegetables, to ensure a good balance of vitamins and minerals.

Many children refuse to eat cooked vegetables – mainly because of their different texture – but will happily try raw sticks of carrot, red pepper and celery or lightly steamed mangetout, baby sweetcorn and broccoli, especially if dipped in houmus, guacamole, garlic butter or mayonnaise. Presenting vegetables in various guises also seems to work and makes them more acceptable to fussy young eaters. Try disguising vegetables by puréeing them in soups and sauces, combining them with mashed potatoes or grating them into meat or vegetarian patties or burgers.

Meat, fish, eggs and vegetarian alternatives

Your toddler requires some of these protein foods at every main meal, but it is vital to offer a good variety, including beans, lentils and soya-based foods. Protein foods are essential for growth and development and are also incredibly versatile, lending themselves to a variety of dishes.

Dairy foods

Milk, cheese and yogurt provide protein, vitamins and minerals, particularly calcium for healthy bones and teeth. Although cow's milk can be used in cooking from 6 months, it's suitable as a drink from 1 year. Opt for full-cream dairy produce because it provides the fat and therefore the energy required by your growing child. You can switch to semi-skimmed milk from 5 years. Experts recommend that children under 5 have 600 ml/1 pint of milk a day, although some of this can be poured over breakfast cereals or offered in the form of sauces and milky puddings.

Sugary foods

Young children naturally have a sweet tooth and it's easy to pander to this preference. Unfortunately, sugary foods, including chocolate, sweets, cakes, biscuits and fizzy drinks, rot the teeth and spoil a child's appetite for healthier alternatives. It can be a challenge to curb a child's desire for sweet foods, especially when presented with aisles of sugary delights while food shopping, but try to start as you mean to go on. Look for healthier alternatives to the above, but don't resort to those containing artificial sweeteners, since they've been found to cause upset stomachs if eaten in excess. Nevertheless, an outright ban on sweet foods can backfire, making them even more desirable to your toddler: as in most things, the answer seems to be to offer sugary things in moderation and perhaps as treats when your child has been good.

Fatty foods

Children need a higher proportion of fat in their diets than adults, both for energy and development. This does not mean that children thrive on high-fat pastries, biscuits, cakes, crisps and fried foods, but do try, at least up to the age of 5, to offer full-fat dairy products, oils of vegetable origin, lean meat, skinless chicken and oily fish such as salmon, tuna, mackerel, sardines and herrings. Avoid hydrogenated fats, found in many processed foods, including pies, sausages and biscuits, since they are just as bad for us as saturated fats. Grilling, poaching and baking foods are preferable.

Salty foods

Cut down on salt as much as possible, especially as this seasoning is found naturally in many foods and is also added to many commercial products. If cooking for the whole family, remove your child's portion before adding any salt.

ABOVE *Your child will become increasingly active and have high energy levels.*

Establishing a Routine

All toddlers are different – some take to eating three main meals a day, others prefer to snack. Both are acceptable at this stage, although, as your toddler becomes older, it is advisable to introduce a pattern of regular eating times. Try to make mealtimes fun and not a time of conflict.

Three meals a day

Work on establishing a regular eating pattern, based on three main meals, plus a couple of snacks a day. Even this can take time and patience to establish, however, so don't despair. If 'grazing' is preferred by your toddler, make sure that he or she is offered a varied selection of healthy snacks (see page 83) based on high-energy foods.

Toddlers have small stomachs and require regular small meals to keep them going. Don't worry if he or she sometimes doesn't seem hungry, or even skips a meal: as long as your toddler is gaining weight and also growing and developing well, then there should be no need for concern. A healthy diet should be based on fruits and vegetables, bread, pasta, rice, potatoes, breakfast cereals, meat, fish, eggs and full-fat dairy produce, with the occasional sweet treat. You may obviously have to make allowances for personal preferences and special diets. There is now no need to purée or mash foods – your toddler should be getting used to, or be familiar with, chewing and with the sometimes unfamiliar texture of solid foods. Some young children dislike lumps, whether meat, fruit or vegetables, and mincing or finely chopping such foods may make them acceptable.

Presentation

Imaginative and attractive presentation can make the difference between a toddler eating or refusing to even try a meal. As with initial weaning try to vary colours, shapes and textures. It can make all the difference. Using brightly coloured plates, cups and cutlery can also help, as can a colourful tablecloth and napkins. Dressing up for mealtimes can also make them seem exciting.

ABOVE *Replace some of your child's milk intake with home-made fruit smoothies or unsweetened fruit juice.*

Drinks

Milk should still form an important part of your child's diet, since it provides a valuable combination of energy, protein, calcium, iron, zinc and vitamins. Cola, fizzy drinks, tea, coffee and sweetened fruit juices and squash should be avoided if possible. Sugar-laden drinks rot the teeth, curb the appetite and lead to weight gain. However, low-sugar alternatives that contain artificial sweeteners are often no better, and can upset the stomach if drunk in excess. Water, diluted unsweetened fruit juices and home-made versions are the preferred option. Smoothies, made from puréed fruit, milk and/or yogurt, freshly squeezed juices and home-made hot chocolate (cubes of good-quality chocolate melted into hot milk) all make nutritious, comforting drinks that are not full of sugar and additives.

MEAL PLANNER 5

18-36 MONTHS	BREAKFAST	LUNCH	TEA	SUPPER
Day 1	Ready Brek, toast, milk	Creamy smoked salmon & broccoli pasta Baked peach crumbles	Pizza fingers Houmus & vegetable sticks Yogurt	Sardines on toast Fruit Milky drink
Day 2	Boiled egg, toast, melon, milk	Spicy rice balls with tomato sauce Vegetables Banana custard scrunch	Crispy chicken fingers with garlic dip Strawberry & vanilla yogurt ice	Cheese on toast Fruit Milky drink
Day 3	Weetabix and banana Fruit bread, milk	Starfish pie, peas Baked apple & custard	Hearty bean & pasta soup Garlic bread Mini chocolate and banana muffin	Sandwich Fruit Milky drink
Day 4	Porridge & grated apple Toast, milk	Pork & apple casserole Potatoes & vegetables Fromage frais	Baked potato with tuna & sweetcorn Strawberry ice lolly	Scrambled egg with muffin Fruit & milky drink
Day 5	Pancakes with fruit filling Yogurt, milk	Bubble & squeak patties Peas and grilled sausage Ice cream	Eggy bread and beans Flapjack	Guacamole with tortilla/pitta bread Vegetable sticks Fruit & milky drink
Day 6	Cereal & raisins, toast, milk	Pasta and vegetables in cheese sauce Baked peach crumbles	Rice balls/chicken sticks with houmus and tortilla Crunchy nut coleslaw Strawberry yogurt ice	Sandwich Fruit Milky drink
Day 7	Diced bacon & grilled tomatoes on toast Yogurt, milk	Roast (or vegetarian alternative), roast potatoes and vegetables Rice pudding with raisins	Tuna and cheese on toast Vegetable sticks Banana custard scrunch	Apple muffins Fruit Milky drink

Hearty Bean & Pasta Soup

PREPARATION TIME: 10 MINUTES	COOKING TIME: 40 MINUTES
FREEZING: SUITABLE, OMIT PARMESAN CHEESE	SERVES: 4

This wholesome bean and pasta soup is substantial enough to be served as a main meal, providing a good balance of vegetables and pasta. Accompany it with garlic bread.

❶ Heat the olive oil in a large, heavy-based saucepan. Add the onion, celery and carrot and cook over a medium heat for 8–10 minutes, stirring occasionally, until the vegetables have softened.

❷ Add the bay leaf, stock and chopped tomatoes, then bring to the boil. Reduce the heat, cover and simmer for 15 minutes, or until the vegetables just tender.

❸ Add the pasta and beans, then bring the soup back to the boil and

INGREDIENTS:
4 tbsp olive oil
1 onion, finely chopped
1 celery stick, chopped
1 carrot, peeled and diced
1 bay leaf
1.2 litres/2 pints vegetable stock
400 g/14 oz can chopped tomatoes
175 g/6 oz pasta shapes, such as farfalle, shells or twists
400-g/14-oz can cannellini beans, drained and rinsed
salt and freshly ground black pepper
200 g/7 oz spinach or chard, thick stalks removed and shredded
40 g/1½ oz Parmesan cheese, finely grated

cook for 10 minutes, or until the pasta is just tender. Stir occasionally to prevent the pasta sticking to the bottom of the pan and burning.

❹ Season to taste, add the spinach and cook for a further 2 minutes, or until tender. Serve, sprinkled with Parmesan cheese.

Creamy Smoked Salmon & Broccoli Pasta

PREPARATION TIME: 15 MINUTES	COOKING TIME: 25 MINUTES
FREEZING: SUITABLE	SERVES: 2

Smoked salmon pieces are now readily available in supermarkets and fishmongers and don't cost the earth. It is ideal for this dish as it has a milder flavour and loses its oily texture when cooked, which seems to appeal to children.

❶ Cook the pasta according to the instructions on the packet, until the pasta is tender, then drain. Meanwhile, steam the broccoli for 8–10 minutes, or until tender.

❷ At the same time, prepare the sauce. Heat the oil and butter in a small heavy-based frying pan, then add the leek and sauté for 7 minutes, or until softened. Gently stir in the cream cheese and milk and heat through.

INGREDIENTS:
400 g/14 oz pasta shells, bows or tagliatelle
225 g/8 oz broccoli florets
1 tbsp olive oil
2 tbsp butter
1 leek, finely chopped
200 g tub garlic and herb cream cheese
6 tbsp whole milk
100 g/3½ oz smoked salmon pieces
salt and freshly ground black pepper

❸ Add the smoked salmon pieces and cook, until they turn opaque. Combine everything well.

Pizza Fingers

PREPARATION TIME: 15 MINUTES, PLUS PROVING **COOKING TIME:** 25 MINUTES
FREEZING: SUITABLE **SERVES:** 2

This pizza is sliced into handy-sized pieces, which are perfect for little fingers to hold. I've given a choice of four toppings to give the pizza a draughtboard effect, but you can opt for one topping if preferred. Additionally, a ready-made foccacia or ciabatta is a good alternative to a home-made base.

❶ To make the pizza base, place the flour, salt and yeast in a bowl. Make a well in the centre of the flour and add the water and oil, then mix with a knife until the mixture forms a soft dough.

❷ Turn out onto a lightly floured work surface and knead for 5 minutes. Cover and leave for 5 minutes. Knead again for a further 5 minutes until the dough is elastic. Place in a lightly oiled bowl and cover with clingfilm. Leave in a warm place for 45 minutes.

❸ Preheat the oven to 220°C/425°F/Gas Mark 7. To make the tomato sauce, heat the oil in a heavy-based frying pan and fry the garlic for 1 minute. Add the passata and sugar, then cook for 5–7 minutes, until thickened. Stir in the oregano and seasoning; set aside.

INGREDIENTS:
PIZZA BASE
225 g/8 oz strong white flour, sifted
1 tsp salt
½ tsp easy-blend yeast
150 ml/5 fl oz warm water
1 tbsp olive oil, plus extra for greasing and sprinkling
TOMATO SAUCE
2 tsp olive oil
1 clove garlic, crushed
140 g/5 oz passata
½ tsp sugar
½ tsp oregano
salt and freshly ground black pepper
TOPPINGS
Handful of cooked fresh spinach leaves, tough stalks removed, shredded and squeezed dry
75 g/2¾ oz canned tuna in oil, drained
½ yellow or orange pepper, seeded and finely sliced
4 slices salami
115 g/4 oz mozzarella cheese
85 g/3 oz Cheddar cheese, grated

❹ Knead the risen dough lightly, then roll out to form a rough rectangle and place in an oiled rectangular-shaped tin. If you are not using a tin, place the base on a lightly oiled baking sheet and push up the edges of the dough to form a shallow rim.

❺ Spoon the tomato mixture over the base. Top one quarter of the base with the cooked spinach, a second quarter with tuna, a third quarter with the yellow pepper and the remaining quarter with salami. Crumble the mozzarella cheese with your fingers and sprinkle it over the toppings. Repeat with the Cheddar cheese. Season and drizzle with a little olive oil.

❻ Bake in the top of the oven for 12–15 minutes, until the topping is slightly crisp and golden. Slice the pizza into manageable-sized fingers before serving.

Pork & Apple Casserole

PREPARATION TIME: 10 MINUTES **COOKING TIME:** 1 HOUR 18 MINUTES

FREEZING: SUITABLE **SERVES:** 4

The apple adds a delicious sweetness and texture to this warming casserole, packed with tender pork pieces. It is a big hit served with a dollop of mashed potato or plain rice.

❶ Preheat the oven to 180°C/350°F/Gas Mark 4.

❷ Heat the oil in a heavy-based frying pan. Add the pork and cook for 5 minutes, until brown. Transfer to a casserole dish.

❸ Add the leeks to the pan and sauté for 5 minutes, or until softened, then add the carrots. Cook for a further 3 minutes, covered. Add the flour and cook for 1 minute, stirring well.

❹ Add the stock, apple juice, mustard, bay leaf and rosemary. Bring to the boil and cook for 2 minutes. Season to taste.

INGREDIENTS:
1 tbsp olive oil
4 boneless pork loins, each weighing about 115 g/4 oz
2 leeks, finely sliced
2 carrots, peeled and finely chopped
1 tbsp plain flour
200 ml/7 fl oz vegetable stock
75 ml/2½ fl oz apple juice
2 tsp Dijon mustard
1 bay leaf
1 tbsp fresh rosemary, finely chopped
2 eating apples, peeled, cored and sliced
salt and freshly ground black pepper

❺ Arrange the apple slices on top of the pork and pour the sauce over the top. Cover and cook for about 1 hour, or until the pork is tender.

Crispy Chicken Fingers with Garlic Dip

PREPARATION TIME: 15 MINUTES **COOKING TIME:** 8 MINUTES

FREEZING: SUITABLE **SERVES:** 6 FINGERS

These polenta-encrusted chicken pieces are perfect finger food for toddlers, and they enjoy dipping them into the garlic dip! Serve with the crunchy nut coleslaw (see page 58).

❶ First make the garlic dip. Put the mayonnaise, garlic and lemon juice into a bowl and mix well.

❷ Put the cornmeal, paprika and seasoning in a shallow bowl. Dip each piece of chicken into the olive oil, then the egg. Roll the chicken in the cornmeal mixture and shake to remove any crumbs.

INGREDIENTS:
20 g/¾ oz fine cornmeal or polenta
½ tsp paprika
salt and freshly ground black pepper
175 g/6 oz skinless chicken breast, cut into strips
1 tbsp olive oil
1 egg, beaten
vegetable oil, for shallow frying
GARLIC DIP
6 tbsp mayonnaise
1 small clove garlic, crushed
good squeeze of fresh lemon juice

❸ Heat enough oil to generously cover a heavy-based frying pan. Arrange the chicken in the pan and fry for 2–3 minutes on each side, until cooked and golden.

Starfish Pie

PREPARATION TIME: 10 MINUTES   **COOKING TIME:** 45 MINUTES

FREEZING: SUITABLE   **SERVES:** 4

Golden puff-pastry shapes add a fun element to this creamy fish pie, but you can opt for mashed potato if preferred. It's wise to sift through the pie with a fork before serving to ensure there are no stray bones.

INGREDIENTS:
1 tbsp olive oil
1 onion, finely chopped
1 celery stick, finely chopped
1 carrot, peeled and finely chopped
small handful of spinach leaves, tough stalks removed and finely shredded
250 ml/8 fl oz full-cream milk
4 tbsp double cream
55 g/2 oz mature Cheddar cheese, grated
1 tsp Dijon mustard
2 tbsp finely chopped fresh parsley
squeeze of fresh lemon juice
salt and freshly ground black pepper
225 g/8 oz undyed smoked haddock, skin and bones removed, cut into pieces
225 g/8 oz cod fillet, skin and bones removed
2 hard-boiled eggs
1 sheet of ready-rolled puff pastry, defrosted if using frozen
1 egg, beaten, to glaze

❶ Preheat the oven to 200°C/400°F/Gas Mark 6.

❷ Heat the oil in a heavy-based frying pan. Add the onion and sauté for 5 minutes, or until softened, then add the celery and carrot and sauté for 3 minutes. Add the spinach and cook for a further 2 minutes, or until tender.

❸ Stir in the milk and cream and bring to the boil. Turn off the heat and stir in the Cheddar cheese, mustard, parsley and lemon juice. Season to taste.

❹ Place the fish in an ovenproof dish. Peel and chop the eggs and spoon them over the fish, then top with the creamy vegetable sauce.

❺ Place the pastry on a lightly floured work surface. Make fish and starfish shapes using biscuit cutters, then arrange them on top of the fish pie. Brush the pastry shapes with beaten egg and bake for 20–25 minutes, or until the fish is cooked and the pastry shapes have risen and are a golden brown colour.

Crunchy Nut Coleslaw

PREPARATION TIME: 10 MINUTES	**COOKING TIME:** 1 MINUTE
FREEZING: UNSUITABLE	**SERVES:** 2

The natural sweetness of the fruit in this pretty pink salad makes it appealing to toddlers. The spring onion is optional and can be added if your child likes it. The coleslaw goes particularly well with the chicken fingers (page 56).

❶ Mix together the ingredients for the dressing in a small bowl.

❷ Place the sunflower seeds in a dry frying pan and cook for a minute or so until they are a light golden brown colour.

❸ Put the cabbage, carrot, apple and spring onion, if using, in a serving bowl. Add the sunflower seeds and mix until all the ingredients are combined.

❹ Spoon over the dressing and stir to coat the salad.

INGREDIENTS:
2 tbsp sunflower seeds
½ small red cabbage, grated
1 large carrot, peeled and grated
½ apple, cored and diced
1 spring onion, finely sliced (optional)
DRESSING
3 tbsp mayonnaise
1 tsp white wine vinegar, according to taste
2 tbsp natural yogurt
salt and freshly ground black pepper

Bubble & Squeak Patties

PREPARATION TIME: 15 MINUTES	**COOKING TIME:** 40 MINUTES
FREEZING: SUITABLE	**SERVES:** 4

These patties are a great way of getting children to eat cabbage! They are delicious with a fresh tomato sauce.

❶ Cook the potatoes in salted boiling water for 15 minutes, or until tender. Drain well.

❷ Meanwhile, steam the cabbage for 5–8 minutes, or until tender.

❸ While the potatoes and cabbage are cooking, heat the oil in a heavy-based frying pan. Fry the onion for 5–8 minutes.

❹ Place the potatoes and cabbage in a large bowl and mash using a potato masher. Add the onion, mustard, Cheddar, egg and seasoning and mix well with a wooden spoon until all the ingredients are combined. Leave until cool enough to handle.

INGREDIENTS:
700 g/1 lb 9 oz potatoes, peeled and cut into even-sized pieces
300 g/10½ oz Savoy or green cabbage, finely shredded
1 tbsp olive oil
1 onion, finely chopped
1 tsp Dijon mustard
85 g/3 oz mature Cheddar cheese, grated
1 egg, beaten
salt and freshly ground black pepper
flour, for dusting
vegetable oil, for frying

❺ Flour a large plate and your hands and shape the mixture into 8 patties. Heat enough oil to cover the base of a large frying pan and fry the patties in batches over a medium heat for 3–4 minutes on each side.

Spicy Rice Balls with Tomato Sauce

PREPARATION TIME: 15 MINUTES PLUS 30 COOLING	
COOKING TIME: 30 MINUTES **FREEZING:** SUITABLE **SERVES:** 4	

These delicately spiced rice balls are similar to falafel but have a lighter texture. I've used arborio rice because its sticky texture helps the balls hold together, but any type of cooked rice is suitable for this recipe. You can also serve them wrapped in a warm tortilla with houmus.

INGREDIENTS:

85 g/3 oz arborio rice

300 ml/10 fl oz vegetable stock

1 tbsp olive oil

1 onion, finely chopped

2 cloves garlic, finely chopped

1 tsp ground cumin

1 tsp ground coriander

½ tsp paprika

200 g/7 oz canned chickpeas, drained and rinsed

1 egg, beaten

fine cornmeal or polenta, for coating

3–4 tbsp sesame seeds

sunflower oil, for frying

TOMATO SAUCE

1 tbsp olive oil

1 clove garlic, finely chopped

1 glass white wine (optional)

400 g/14 oz passata

2 tsp tomato purée

½ tsp sugar

salt and freshly ground black pepper

❶ Place the rice in a saucepan and cover with the stock, stirring well. Bring to the boil, then reduce the heat and simmer, covered, for 15–20 minutes, or until the water has been absorbed and the rice is tender. Remove from the heat and leave the saucepan to sit, covered, for 5 minutes. Drain well and allow to cool for 30 minutes.

❷ To make the tomato sauce, heat the oil in a heavy-based saucepan and sauté the garlic for 1 minute, or until softened. Add the wine, if using, and cook over a high heat for a minute or so, until the alcohol has evaporated. Reduce the heat to medium, add the passata, tomato purée and sugar and cook for 15 minutes, or until the sauce has reduced and thickened. Season.

❸ Meanwhile, make the rice balls. Heat the olive oil in a heavy-based frying pan. Add the onion and fry for 5–7 minutes, or until softened. Add the garlic and spices and cook for 1 minute, stirring. Stir in the rice, chickpeas and the beaten egg.

❹ Transfer the rice, chickpea, egg and onion mixture to a blender. Season to taste and process until thick and fairly smooth.

❺ Cover a large plate with a layer of cornmeal and sprinkle over the sesame seeds. For each rice ball, take a walnut-sized amount of the rice mixture and form it into a ball, then roll it in the cornmeal and sesame seed mixture. Repeat until you have used all the rice mixture.

❻ Heat enough oil to cover the base of a frying pan, then cook the rice balls for 4 minutes, turning occasionally, until crisp and golden. (You will have to cook the balls in batches.) Drain the rice balls on kitchen paper to mop up any excess oil.

❼ To serve, divide the tomato sauce between 4 shallow bowls, then arrange the rice balls on top.

Banana Custard Scrunch

PREPARATION TIME: 5 MINUTES	COOKING TIME: 3 MINUTES
FREEZING: UNSUITABLE	SERVES: 4

Layers of honey-coated oats, bananas and yogurt custard taste indulgent but couldn't be easier to make. Children love it when the scrunch is served in tall glasses with a long spoon.

❶ Mix together the yogurt and custard in a bowl.

❷ Put the oats in a dry frying pan and toast them for a minute. Add the honey and stir well to coat the oats. Cook for 2 minutes over a medium heat, stirring, until the oats become golden and slightly crisp at the edges.

❸ To serve, spoon the oat mixture, reserving a little to decorate, into the bottom of 4 glasses or

INGREDIENTS:
300 g/10½ oz thick natural yogurt
200 g/7 oz ready-made custard
70 g/2½ oz porridge oats
2 tbsp runny honey
2–3 bananas, sliced

ramekins. Arrange two-thirds of the banana over the oats, then top with the yogurt custard. Top with the bananas and sprinkle with oats.

Strawberry & Vanilla Yogurt Ice

PREPARATION TIME: 20 MINUTES	
FREEZING: SUITABLE	SERVES: 4

Yogurt adds a refreshing tang to this home-made fresh fruit ice, which can be scooped into small cones – the perfect size for toddlers of this age. Live yogurt is beneficial to the digestive system and can help to fight off stomach upsets. As an added bonus, this ice is free from additives and stabilisers.

❶ Whisk together the yogurt and mascarpone in a bowl. Pour into a shallow, freezer-proof container and freeze for 1 hour.

❷ Purée the strawberries and vanilla essence in a blender until smooth, then mix with the honey.

❸ Remove the semi-frozen yogurt mixture from the freezer and fold in the strawberry and honey mixture. Beat the mixture well.

INGREDIENTS:
350 g/12 oz thick live natural yogurt
200 g/7 oz mascarpone cheese
450 g/1 lb strawberries, hulled and sliced
1 tsp vanilla essence
6 tbsp runny honey

❹ Return the yogurt ice to the freezer and freeze for a further 2 hours. Remove from the freezer and beat again, then freeze until solid. Serve in scoops with strawberries.

Baked Peach Crumbles

PREPARATION TIME: 15 MINUTES **COOKING TIME:** 30 MINUTES

FREEZING: SUITABLE **SERVES:** 4

These individual crumbles are especially delicious with a dollop of custard or ice cream.

❶ Preheat the oven to 180°C/350°F/Gas Mark 4.

❷ Arrange the peach halves in the bottom of a small, lightly greased ovenproof dish.

❸ Put the flour and butter in a bowl and rub together with your fingertips to form coarse breadcrumbs. Stir in the oats and sugar and mix well.

❹ Sprinkle generous amounts of the crumble mixture over the peach

INGREDIENTS:
4 peaches, halved and stoned
40 g/1½ oz plain flour, sifted
2 tbsp butter, plus extra for greasing
2 tbsp porridge oats
3 tbsp light brown sugar

TIP Add 1 tbsp of chopped mixed nuts and 1 tbsp finely chopped dried dates to the crumble mixture.

halves. Bake for 25–30 minutes, or until the peaches are tender and the crumble mixture is crisp and golden.

Mini Chocolate & Banana Muffins

PREPARATION TIME: 10 MINUTES **COOKING TIME:** 15 MINUTES

FREEZING: SUITABLE **SERVES:** 24 SMALL MUFFINS

These muffins are a good size for toddlers and are delicious, especially when warm and the chocolate is still gooey.

❶ Preheat the oven to 200°C/400°F/Gas Mark 6. Butter 2 x 12-hole small bun tins.

❷ Sift together the flour, salt and baking powder in a large bowl. Add the sugar and chocolate to the flour mixture and then stir.

❸ Place the milk, eggs, butter and yogurt in a separate bowl and whisk until combined. Add the egg mixture to the flour mixture, stirring until just combined, but don't overmix or it will result in heavy muffins.

❹ Gently fold the mashed bananas into the mixture.

INGREDIENTS:
140 g/5 oz plain flour
pinch of salt
1 tsp baking powder
140 g/5 oz light muscovado sugar
115 g/4 oz milk chocolate, broken into chunks
3 tbsp milk
2 eggs, beaten
140 g/5 oz unsalted butter, melted
3 tbsp low-fat natural yogurt
2 small bananas, mashed

❺ Spoon the mixture into the greased bun tins or paper cake cases and bake for 12–15 minutes, or until risen and slightly golden. Leave in the tin for 5 minutes, then turn out on to a wire rack to cool.

THREE TO FOUR YEARS

Your toddler will by now be happily practising his or her eating skills, which can be a messy affair but nevertheless a crucial stage in a child's development. Accept and be prepared for the mess and try to resist the temptation to intervene too much. Alongside developing his or her own individuality, your 3 to 4-year-old will also become increasingly affected by outside influences, especially if he or she attends a playgroup or nursery.

Nutritional Needs

The nutritional requirements of 3 to 4-year-olds are not that different from those of an 18-month-old. Although by this age the rate of growth has slowed down considerably, 3 to 4-year-olds are generally more active and their diets need to compensate for this increase in energy levels. High-energy foods still need to be included in your toddler's diet.

ABOVE *Your child's likes and dislikes may be influenced by the nursery food that they are offered.*

All small children require sufficient calories and a variety of foods (based on the major food groups mentioned on pages 50–51) to enable them to fuel their high energy levels. They also need to be encouraged to enjoy the pleasures of eating and good food. This sounds simple in theory but good intentions can backfire in practice (see 'Coping with a fussy eater'). Do stick to your guns, however, and rest assured that by providing plenty of fresh, unprocessed foods you are doing the best for your child's health and development in the long term despite the protests your child might make. Nutritionists suggest that a varied, healthy diet can help to curb the major diseases that plague us in the West later in life, and there is also evidence to show that a good diet can help to relieve the symptoms of asthma.

Outside influences

Many 3 to 4-year-olds attend a playgroup or nursery and with this comes its own challenges. You may be fortunate to find an ideal establishment that serves a variety of freshly prepared, nutritious lunches, snacks and healthy drinks. Realistically, food standards tend to vary and it can be awkward for parents to ask for changes without appearing difficult and demanding.

Many nurseries are open to parents providing their own drinks, snacks and packed lunches and this may be a welcome option. Alternatively, take the softly-softly approach, arming yourself with relevant information, articles and books and talking to the people who run the nursery or playgroup. Often a lack of knowledge is to blame for poor food quality and all that is needed is a little encouragement.

Eating out

It can be a challenge to find a restaurant that not only welcomes children with open arms but also provides decent healthy food. Most children's menus offer the usual repertoire of fish fingers and chips, burger and chips, and sausage and chips, followed by poor-quality ice cream and jelly. There is also the further lure of a free gift! Consequently, all your good intentions fly out of the window as your children clamour for the food.

Most children love the novelty of eating out and, from experience, the better quality pizza chains, Italian, Indian and Chinese restaurants offer the best choice and are often more welcoming to families with young children. Alternatively, choose a starter from the main menu or ask for a separate plate and share your meal. Sometimes the chef may provide a small child-sized portion of a main course.

Eating out can be a hit-or-miss affair, and it is best to pick a time when your little one is not very tired and choose a restaurant that is not too formal, where it may be difficult to relax. To prevent occasional boredom, take along pens and paper or a small toy to keep your child entertained, and try not force your child to eat. Even a mouthful of a new food is progress!

Coping With a Fussy Eater

All toddlers go through stages of picky eating and their appetites can be equally unpredictable. However frustrating this may be, try not to let this trouble you. There are plenty of stories of toddlers surviving on nothing but toast and jam for some unimaginable amount of time – remarkably, most don't seem to suffer adverse effects.

How do you encourage your child to eat what you want him or her to, and what do you do if he or she refuses to eat at all? There are no easy answers, but the following guidelines should help you cope more easily with those challenging times:

• Don't force your child to eat. Conflict and tension serve only to make the situation worse and may lead to your child using mealtimes as a way of seeking attention. Children are remarkably clever at picking up on the anxieties of their parents and may well pick up on your own insecurities about food. Instead, try to gently coax or encourage your child to try a little bit of what you have prepared. I've found that my daughter will happily eat a meal once I've encouraged her to try 'just a mouthful'.

• If your gentle coaxing doesn't work, remove the food without making a fuss, but don't offer an alternative dish, however hard this may be. I know, speaking as someone who has prepared numerous alternatives when my daughter has refused to eat, that this is a losing battle. Your child is unlikely to starve and it's important that they learn to eat what's on offer, rather than expect you to provide endless alternatives.

• Don't overload your child's plate. Small amounts of food tend to be more acceptable to small stomachs.

• Praise and encourage your child as much as possible, even if they eat only a mouthful of what you have prepared.

• Make eating fun. Picnics, even if it's only a cloth arranged on the kitchen floor, games, or basing a meal on a theme, such as a favourite cartoon character, book or season, can be a real success.

ABOVE *Presenting small portions of food to your toddler is less off-putting and seems more manageable.*

• Try to ignore poor eating habits and complaints such as 'yuck', however hard and upsetting this may be.

• Ask a friend of your child's, who you know to be a good eater, to come to tea. Children often learn by example and may be encouraged to eat by their peers. Beware, this can sometimes backfire – my daughter hasn't eaten peas since a friend said she disliked them!

• Don't fall into the trap of bribing your child with a pudding, and then giving it even if the main meal remains uneaten. This will only help to discourage good eating habits.

• Compromise is sometimes the only way to get your child to eat certain things. Combine foods that you know your child likes with others that are untried or previously rejected.

MEAL PLANNER 1

3–4 YEARS	BREAKFAST	LUNCH	TEA	SUPPER
Day 1	Diced bacon & grilled tomatoes Toast, yogurt	Pasta bolognese, broccoli Fruit salad	Surf 'n' turf paella Ice cream sundae	Guacamole with pitta bread Vegetable sticks Fruit & milky drink
Day 2	Porridge, fruit, toast	Bacon, pea & potato frittata, coleslaw Baked apple and custard	Chinese noodles Banana custard scrunch	Tortilla parcel Fruit & milky drink
Day 3	Cereal/muesli, muffin	Creamy tomato & lentil soup Garlic bread with cheese Chocolate muffin	Golden fish fingers with sweet potato wedges and peas Strawberry yogurt ice	Sardines on toast Fruit & milky drink
Day 4	Poached egg & beans Toast Yogurt	Higgledy-piggledy pie with potatoes and vegetables Ice cream strawberry sundae	Crispy chicken fingers, coleslaw Baked potato Fromage frais & fruit	Cheese on toast Fruit & milky drink
Day 5	Cereal, toast	Starfish pie with French beans Fruity chocolate bread pudding	Spicy rice balls with tomato sauce, vegetables Yogurt	Sandwich Fruit & milky drink
Day 6	Pancake with stewed apple Yogurt	Pork & apple casserole Potatoes & vegetables Baked peach crumbles	Smoked salmon & broccoli pasta Flapjack	Houmus/cheese tortilla Vegetable sticks Fruit & milky drink
Day 7	Cheese scrambled eggs on toast Fruit	Winter sausage hot pot Vegetables Sandcastle cakes	Baked potato with pesto & cheese Buttermilk pancakes with hot maple bananas	Fruit & milky drink

Creamy Tomato & Lentil Soup

PREPARATION TIME: 10 MINUTES	COOKING TIME: 45 MINUTES
FREEZING: SUITABLE	SERVES: 4

Remarkably, children who turn their noses up at vegetables will happily eat them when liquidised into a soup. Most toddlers love tomato soup, and this one is free from the additives often found in manufactured alternatives. The lentils add extra goodness and substance, but they can be swapped for beans or cooked rice. I usually serve this soup with mini cheese toasts, although croûtons, garlic bread or a hunk of crusty bread are just as good.

INGREDIENTS:
55 g/2 oz split red lentils, rinsed
1 tbsp olive oil
1 onion, chopped
1 carrot, peeled and finely chopped
1 celery stick, chopped
500 g/1 lb 2 oz carton creamed tomatoes
600 ml/1 pint vegetable stock
cream or natural yogurt, to serve (optional)
salt and freshly ground black pepper
CHEESE TOASTS
8 slices French bread
butter, for spreading
55 g/2 oz Gruyère or mature Cheddar cheese, grated
½ tsp dried oregano

❶ Place the lentils in a saucepan, cover with water and bring to the boil. Reduce the heat and simmer, half covered, for 25 minutes, or until tender. Drain the lentils well and set them aside.

❷ While the lentils are cooking, make the soup. Heat the oil in a heavy-based saucepan. Add the onion, cover the pan and sweat for 10 minutes, or until softened and transparent. Add the carrot and celery and sweat the vegetables for a further 2 minutes, stirring occasionally to prevent the vegetables sticking to the bottom of the pan and burning.

❸ Add the creamed tomatoes and stock and bring to the boil. Reduce the heat and simmer, half covered, for 25 minutes, or until the vegetables are tender and the liquid has reduced and thickened. Add the lentils to the pan.

❹ Carefully pour the mixture into a blender and blend until it is smooth and creamy. Return the soup to the pan, season to taste and heat through gently if necessary. Swirl a spoonful of cream, if using, over the soup and serve.

❺ For the cheese toasts, preheat the grill to high. Lightly toast the French bread on one side. Butter the untoasted side and sprinkle with the Gruyère cheese and oregano. Grill until golden.

Golden Fish Fingers with Sweet Potato Wedges

PREPARATION TIME: 15 MINUTES	**COOKING TIME:** 35 MINUTES
FREEZING: SUITABLE	**SERVES:** 8–10 FINGERS

If making your own fish fingers sounds like too much effort, this simple, quick version may change your mind, and you can also guarantee the quality of the ingredients used. The cod fillets are covered in a crisp, golden crumb, made from fresh breadcrumbs, and I like to serve them with these sweet potato wedges.

❶ Preheat the oven to 200°C/400°F/Gas Mark 6.

❷ Dry the sweet potato wedges on a clean tea towel. Place the oil in a roasting tin and heat for a few minutes in the oven. Arrange the potatoes in the tin and bake for 30–35 minutes, turning them halfway through, until they are tender and golden.

❸ Meanwhile, cut the cod into strips, about 2 cm/¾ in wide.

❹ Season the flour and add the paprika. Roll the cod strips in the seasoned flour until coated, shaking off any excess, then dip them in the beaten egg. Roll the cod strips in the breadcrumbs until evenly coated.

❺ Heat enough oil to cover the base of a large, non-stick frying pan. Carefully arrange the fish fingers in the pan – you may have to cook them in batches – and fry them for 3–4 minutes on each side, or until crisp and golden. Drain on kitchen paper before serving, if necessary.

❻ Serve the fish fingers with the sweet potato wedges and peas. Replace ketchup with homemade tomato sauce.

INGREDIENTS:
280 g/10 oz thick cod fillets, skin and bones removed
flour, for dusting
1 tsp paprika
1 egg, beaten
fresh breadcrumbs or fine cornmeal, for coating
sunflower oil, for frying
salt and freshly ground black pepper
SWEET POTATO WEDGES
450 g/1 lb sweet potatoes, scrubbed and cut into wedges
1 tbsp olive oil

Surf 'n' Turf Paella

| PREPARATION TIME: 15 MINUTES | COOKING TIME: 30 MINUTES |
| FREEZING: SUITABLE | SERVES: 2–3 |

This golden rice dish is infused with saffron, but you can use turmeric instead, which gives a similar sunshine colour. Paella rice is perfect for young children as it has a tender, melt-in-the-mouth texture when cooked.

❶ Heat the oil in a large heavy-based sauté pan (with a lid). Add the onion and fry for 5 minutes, or until softened. Add the chicken breast, pepper and garlic and sauté for 5 minutes over a medium heat, stirring frequently to prevent the mixture sticking.

❷ Add the tomato, tomato purée, saffron and stock to the pan. Stir in the rice and bring to the boil, then reduce the heat. Simmer the rice, covered, for 15 minutes, or until the rice is tender.

❸ Add the peas, prawns and seasoning and cook for a further 2–3 minutes, or until the prawns have heated through.

INGREDIENTS:
2 tbsp olive oil
1 onion, diced
2 skinless chicken breasts, sliced
1 small red pepper, seeded and diced
2 cloves garlic, chopped
1 tomato, seeded and chopped
1 tbsp tomato purée
pinch of saffron
600 ml/1 pint hot chicken or vegetable stock
175 g/6 oz paella rice
55 g/2 oz frozen peas
115 g/4 oz cooked prawns, defrosted if frozen
salt and freshly ground black pepper

Pasta Bolognese

PREPARATION TIME: 10 MINUTES	COOKING TIME: 30 MINUTES
FREEZING: SUITABLE	SERVES: 4

Spaghetti is a real favourite with toddlers, who love the slurping and the accompanying mess – so be prepared! Vegetarians can opt for soya mince or Quorn instead of meat. Use good-quality mince if you decide to opt for the meat-eater's version.

❶ Heat the oil in a heavy-based, non-stick saucepan. Add the onion and sauté, half covered, for 5 minutes, or until softened. Add the garlic, carrot and mushrooms, if using, and sauté for a further 3 minutes, stirring occasionally.

❷ Add the herbs and mince to the pan and cook until the meat has browned, stirring regularly.

❸ Add the wine, if using, and cook over a high heat until the alcohol has evaporated, then add the stock and passata. Reduce the heat, season to taste and cook over a low–medium heat, half covered, for 15–20 minutes, or until the sauce has reduced and thickened. Remove the bay leaf.

❹ Meanwhile, cook the pasta according to the instructions on the packet, until the pasta is tender. Drain well and mix together the pasta and sauce until the pasta is well coated.

INGREDIENTS:
2 tbsp olive oil
1 onion, finely chopped
2 cloves garlic, finely chopped
1 carrot, peeled and finely chopped
85 g/3 oz mushrooms, peeled and sliced or chopped (optional)
1 tsp dried oregano
½ tsp dried thyme
1 bay leaf
280 g/10 oz lean mince
1 glass white wine (optional)
300 ml/10 fl oz stock
300 ml/10 fl oz passata
salt and freshly ground black pepper
350 g/12 oz spaghetti or pasta of your choice

Bacon, Pea & Potato Frittata

PREPARATION TIME: 15 MINUTES	**COOKING TIME:** 20 MINUTES
FREEZING: UNSUITABLE	**SERVES:** 3–4

This frittata is similar to the Spanish tortilla. Serve it cut into wedges or fingers, with crusty bread and green vegetables or a salad. This is a good food for small fingers to handle.

INGREDIENTS:

2–3 slices good-quality bacon

1½ tbsp olive oil

1 small onion, finely chopped

350 g/12 oz new potatoes, cooked, halved or quartered, if large

55 g/2 oz frozen petit pois

6 free range eggs, lightly beaten

salt and freshly ground black pepper

❶ Preheat the grill to high. Grill the bacon until crisp. Allow to cool slightly, then cut into small pieces and set aside.

❷ Heat the oil in a large heavy-based, ovenproof frying pan, add the onion and sauté for 5 minutes, or until softened and tender, stirring occasionally.

❸ Add the potatoes and cook for a further 5 minutes, or until golden, stirring to prevent them sticking to the pan. Add the bacon pieces and petit pois, and spread the mixture evenly over the base of the pan.

❹ Reheat the grill to high. Season the beaten eggs, then pour them carefully over the onion and potato mixture. Cook over a moderate heat for 5–6 minutes, or until the eggs are just set and the base of the frittata is lightly golden brown.

❺ Place the pan under the grill and cook the top for 3 minutes, or until set and lightly golden. Serve the frittata warm or cold, cut into wedges or fingers.

Chinese Noodles

PREPARATION TIME: 10 MINUTES PLUS 1 HOUR MARINATING	
COOKING TIME: 20 MINUTES	**FREEZING:** UNSUITABLE	**SERVES:** 4

Toddlers seem to love noodles as much as pasta and this stir-fry is no exception. I've chosen brightly coloured vegetables for maximum appeal, but experiment with different types. Whatever you choose, they are at their best when still slightly crunchy.

❶ Mix together the ingredients for the marinade in a shallow dish. Add the tofu and spoon the marinade over. Refrigerate for 1 hour to marinate, turning the tofu occasionally to allow the flavours to infuse.

❷ Preheat the oven to 200°C/400°F/Gas Mark 6. Using a slotted spoon, remove the tofu from the marinade and reserve the liquid. Arrange the tofu on a baking sheet and roast for 20 minutes, turning occasionally, until the tofu pieces are golden and crisp on all sides.

❸ Meanwhile, cook the noodles in plenty of salted boiling water according to the instructions on the packet, until the noodles are tender, then drain. Rinse the noodles under cold running water and drain again.

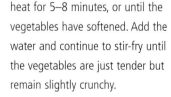

INGREDIENTS:
250 g pack of tofu, cubed
250 g/9 oz medium egg noodles
1 tbsp peanut or vegetable oil
1 red pepper, seeded and sliced
225 g/8 oz broccoli florets
175 g/6 oz baby sweetcorn, halved lengthways
2–3 tbsp water
2 spring onions, finely sliced
1 tbsp sesame seeds, toasted (optional)
MARINADE
1 clove garlic, finely chopped
2.5-cm/1-in piece fresh root ginger, peeled and grated
1 tsp sesame oil
1 tbsp runny honey
2 tbsp dark soy sauce

❹ Heat a wok or heavy-based frying pan, then add the oil. Add the pepper, broccoli and sweetcorn and stir-fry, tossing and stirring continuously, over a medium-high heat for 5–8 minutes, or until the vegetables have softened. Add the water and continue to stir-fry until the vegetables are just tender but remain slightly crunchy.

❺ Stir in the marinade, noodles, tofu and spring onions, and stir-fry until heated through.

❻ Serve sprinkled with sesame seeds, if using.

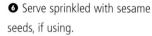

Winter Sausage Hot Pot

PREPARATION TIME: 15 MINUTES	**COOKING TIME:** 45 MINUTES
FREEZING: SUITABLE	**SERVES:** 4

A satisfying, warming stew, which has a savoury scone topping and can be made with either pork or vegetarian sausages. The alcohol in the wine evaporates during cooking.

INGREDIENTS:
6 pork or vegetarian sausages
1 tbsp olive oil
1 onion, chopped
1 clove garlic, chopped
1 celery stick, finely chopped
1 red pepper, seeded and diced
2 courgettes, sliced
2 tsp chopped fresh rosemary
1 tsp thyme
1 bay leaf
1 glass of white wine (optional)
150–300 ml/5–10 fl oz vegetable stock
300 ml/10 fl oz passata
½ tsp sugar
400-g/14-oz can borlotti beans, drained and rinsed
175 g/6 oz self-raising flour, sifted
½ tsp salt
1 heaped tsp baking powder
3 tbsp butter or margarine
50–80 ml/2–3 fl oz milk, plus extra for glazing

❶ Preheat the grill to high. Grill the sausages, turning them occasionally, until they are cooked and golden. Set aside.

❷ Preheat the oven to 200°C/400°F/Gas Mark 6.

❸ Meanwhile, heat the oil in a heavy-based saucepan and sauté the onion, covered, for 5 minutes, or until softened. Add the garlic, celery, pepper, courgettes and herbs and sauté, covered, for a further 5 minutes.

❹ Add the wine, if using, and cook over a medium-high heat for a few minutes until the alcohol has evaporated. If using the wine, add the smaller amount of stock; if not, opt for the greater quantity. Reduce the heat to medium, stir and add the passata and sugar. Stir again and cook for 10 minutes, or until the sauce has reduced.

❺ Slice the cooked sausages and add them to the sauce with the beans. Stir and spoon the mixture into a casserole dish.

❻ To make the scone topping, place the flour, salt and baking powder into a bowl and mix. Add the butter and rub with your fingertips until the mixture forms breadcrumbs.

❼ Gradually stir in the milk using a palette knife and form the mixture into a dough with your floured hands. Knead lightly on a floured work surface until smooth. Take walnut-sized pieces of the dough and roll them into balls. Flatten them and arrange them in a circle on the top.

❽ Brush the top of the scones with milk and bake for 20 minutes, or until the scones have risen.

Higgledy-Piggledy Pie

PREPARATION TIME: 20 MINUTES PLUS THIRTY MINUTES RESTING

COOKING TIME: 55 MINUTES **FREEZING:** SUITABLE **SERVES:** 4

This free-form pie encases a rich tomato, aubergine and kidney bean filling. If your pastry cracks, just patch it up – it adds to the pie's rustic charm. The pastry is enriched with Parmesan cheese, but this can be omitted if desired.

❶ Preheat the oven to 220°C/ 425°F/Gas Mark 7. For the pastry, rub the plain and wholemeal flours, salt and butter together until the mixture resembles fine breadcrumbs, then stir in the Parmesan cheese.

❷ Add enough cold water to form a dough, then turn out the dough on to a lightly floured work surface and knead lightly to form a smooth and elastic dough. Wrap the dough in clingfilm and chill in the refrigerator for 30 minutes.

❸ To make the filling, sprinkle the aubergine with salt and leave for 30 minutes to remove any bitter juices. Rinse and pat dry with kitchen paper.

❹ Heat the oil in a large heavy-based frying pan. Fry the onions for 5 minutes, or until softened, stirring occasionally. Add the pepper and aubergine and fry for 5 minutes, or until tender, then add the courgette, garlic and oregano. Cook for a further 5 minutes. Add the kidney beans, seasoning and chopped tomatoes. Cook for 8 minutes, or until the sauce has reduced and thickened slightly, then cool.

❺ Divide the pastry into four pieces and roll out on a lightly floured work surface to form equal-sized rounds. Place on a lightly greased baking sheet. Brush with egg and sprinkle over the semolina, leaving a 4-cm/1½-in border. Spoon over the filling and sprinkle with cheese.

❻ Gather up the edges of the pastry to partly cover the filling – the pie should remain open in the middle. Brush with egg and bake for 25–30 minutes, or until the pastry is golden.

INGREDIENTS:
450 g/1 lb aubergine, cubed
1 onion, finely chopped
1 red pepper, seeded and diced
2 tbsp olive oil
1 courgette, sliced
2 cloves garlic, crushed
1 tsp dried oregano
200 g/7 oz canned red kidney beans, drained and rinsed
salt and freshly ground black pepper
375 g/13 oz chopped tomatoes
2 tbsp semolina
55 g/2 oz Cheddar cheese, grated
1 egg, beaten, to glaze
PASTRY
½ tsp salt
115 g/4 oz plain flour
115 g/4 oz wholemeal flour
115 g/4 oz butter or vegetable margarine
55 g/2 oz Parmesan cheese, finely grated

Tortilla Parcels

PREPARATION TIME: 5 MINUTES	**COOKING TIME:** 2 MINUTES
FREEZING: UNSUITABLE	**SERVES:** 2 PARCELS

Soft, floury tortillas make a perfect snack or light lunch. These are filled with tuna, mozzarella cheese and diced tomato, but you could vary the filling according to likes and dislikes. Guacamole and houmus are also popular with children and these could be used instead.

❶ Place the mozzarella cheese, tuna, tomato and seasoning along the centre of the tortilla. Fold in the sides, then the ends of the tortilla to encase the filling.

❷ Place the parcel, seam-side down, in a dry, non-stick frying pan and gently warm over a low-medium heat for 2 minutes, turning once, until the tortilla is lightly golden and the filling is warmed through. Cut the tortilla in half and serve immediately.

INGREDIENTS:
4 slices of mozzarella cheese, drained and dried with kitchen paper
2 tbsp canned tuna in oil, drained and mashed
1 small tomato, seeded and diced
salt and freshly ground black pepper
1 soft tortilla

Ice Cream Strawberry Sundae

PREPARATION TIME: 10 MINUTES **COOKING TIME:** 12 MINUTES

FREEZING: SAUCE CAN BE FROZEN **SERVES:** 4

This sumptuous dessert is a real treat, and is enjoyed by adults and children alike! Strawberries are particularly popular with toddlers, and if they are sweet enough you may not need to add extra sugar.

INGREDIENTS:
250 g/9 oz strawberries, hulled and halved
2 tbsp freshly squeezed orange juice
2 tbsp caster sugar
8 scoops of good-quality vanilla ice cream
25 g/1 oz chopped mixed nuts, lightly toasted in a dry frying pan
grated chocolate and marshmallows, to serve

❶ To make the sauce, process the strawberries with the orange juice in a blender until smooth. Transfer the mixture to a saucepan and add the sugar. Cook over a medium heat for 10–12 minutes, or until thickened. Leave to cool.

❷ To serve, place a spoonful of the strawberry sauce in the bottom of a tall glass. Add two scoops of ice cream and another spoonful of fruit sauce. Sprinkle with the nuts. Decorate with the grated chocolate and marshmallows. Repeat for all four sundaes.

VARIATION Replace the strawberry sauce with a rich chocolate sauce. Melt 100 g/3½ oz of good-quality milk chocolate in a bowl, placed over a pan of simmering water. (Make sure the bowl does not touch the water.) Stir very occasionally until melted. Heat 2 tbsp milk, 50 ml/2 fl oz double cream and 2 tbsp caster sugar in a small saucepan and bring to the boil. Gently pour the mixture onto the melted chocolate and whisk until combined and smooth. Serve warm.

Fruity Chocolate Bread Pudding

PREPARATION TIME: 15 MINUTES   **COOKING TIME:** 35 MINUTES

FREEZING: SUITABLE   **SERVES:** 4

A rich, comforting pudding that just melts in the mouth. It is made with fruit bread, but ordinary sliced bread, muffins, brioche or panettone work just as well.

INGREDIENTS:
275 g/9½ oz sliced fruit bread, crusts removed
6 tbsp good-quality chocolate spread
300 ml/10 fl oz milk
½ tsp vanilla essence
1 large free-range egg, beaten
1 tbsp maple syrup
ground cinnamon, for decorating

❶ Preheat the oven to 200°C/400°F/Gas Mark 6. Butter a 25 x 20-cm/10 x 8-in baking dish. Arrange half the fruit bread in the dish in a single layer.

❷ Spread the fruit bread with the chocolate spread. Arrange another layer of fruit bread over the chocolate bread, making sure that it lies flat in the dish.

❸ Gently heat the milk and vanilla essence in a saucepan, until it just reaches boiling point. Remove from the heat and whisk in the egg and maple syrup, mixing well.

❹ Pour the egg mixture over the fruit, lightly pressing down the bread so it is submerged. Leave to soak for 10 minutes.

❺ Bake for 25–30 minutes, or until set and golden. To serve, cut into 4 portions and sprinkle the top of the pudding with ground cinnamon.

Buttermilk Pancakes with Hot Maple Bananas

PREPARATION TIME: 5 MINUTES   COOKING TIME: 5 MINUTES

FREEZING: PANCAKES SUITABLE   SERVES: 4

A simple, very quick and delicious pudding-cum-breakfast.

❶ To make the pancakes, place the flour, salt, sugar and baking powder in a large bowl and mix together.

❷ Mix together the beaten egg, buttermilk and melted butter, then add it to the flour mixture and beat well to remove any lumps.

❸ Heat a teaspoon of the oil in a heavy-based frying pan. Place heaped tablespoons of the batter in the pan and flatten with the back of a spoon. Cook for 3 minutes, or until set and golden, then turn over and cook 2 minutes. Keep warm. Make the remaining pancakes.

❹ Melt the butter in a heavy-based frying pan. Add the bananas and cook for 1 minute over a medium heat, coating them in butter. Add the maple syrup and cook for 1–2 minutes. Spoon over the pancakes.

❺ Add the maple syrup and cook the bananas for 1–2 minutes. To serve, spoon the bananas and syrup over the pancakes.

INGREDIENTS:
140 g/5 oz plain flour, sifted
pinch of salt
2 tbsp caster sugar
1 tsp baking powder
1 egg, beaten
300 ml/10 fl oz carton buttermilk
25 g/1 oz butter, melted
sunflower oil, for frying
3 tbsp unsalted butter
4 bananas, thickly sliced diagonally
6 tbsp maple syrup
1 tbsp flaked almonds, toasted (optional)

Sandcastle Cakes

PREPARATION TIME: 10 MINUTES   COOKING TIME: 20 MINUTES

FREEZING: UNSUITABLE   SERVES: 4 CAKES

These fun, decorated sponge cakes are great for parties or a special teatime treat when your children have been extra good! Top the cakes with home-made flags with each child's name on it for an added fun factor.

❶ Preheat the oven to 180°C/350°F/Gas Mark 4. Lightly grease 4 dariole moulds and line the base with a circle of greaseproof paper.

❷ Sift the flour into a large mixing bowl. Add the sugar, butter and eggs and beat together until smooth and creamy.

❸ Divide the mixture between the moulds, filling them three-quarters full. Place on a baking sheet and cook for 20 minutes, or until risen and golden. Leave for 5 minutes, then turn out to cool.

INGREDIENTS:
115 g/4 oz self-raising flour
115 g/4 oz caster sugar
115 g/4 oz butter or margarine, plus extra for greasing
2 eggs
3 tbsp strawberry jam
silver balls and hundreds and thousands, to decorate

❹ Trim the base of each cake so they stand up. Heat the jam in a saucepan until runny, then brush it over the top and sides of the cakes. Sprinkle or roll the cakes in the hundreds and thousands and decorate with the silver balls.

FOUR PLUS

By this stage, your little one will be making the transition from toddler to young child, and with this comes an increasing independence and free spirit. It is important to allow your child's personality, sense of humour and sense of self to flourish, without knocking his or her confidence if he or she sometimes goes awry. This is especially important at mealtimes, when guidance, gentle persuasion and plenty of patience are vital.

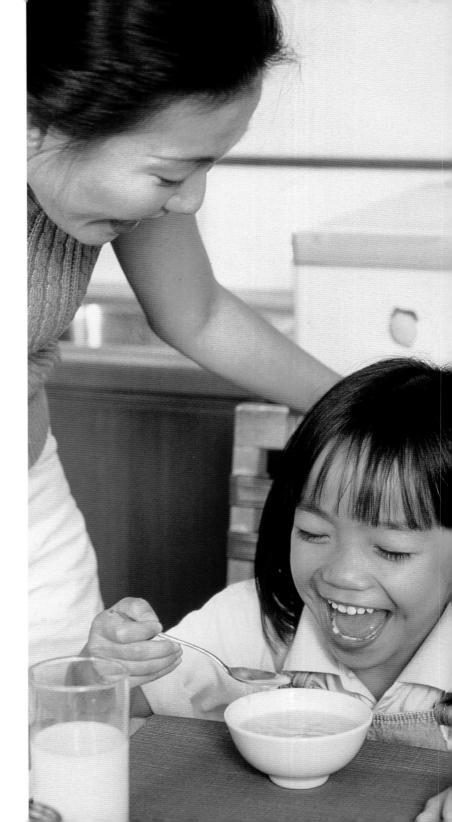

Nutritional Needs

For many young children, their fourth year heralds the start of full-time education. School presents its own challenges and it can be a time when good intentions and eating habits fall by the wayside. However, a nutritious, varied diet is as important as ever – sustaining and boosting energy levels, concentration and, some experts even say, brain power.

Many children do not eat breakfast before they go to school or simply rely on a bag of crisps or a chocolate bar to fight off hunger pangs until lunchtime. Many nutritionists believe that breakfast is the most important meal of the day, replenishing nutrients and energy stocks depleted overnight. High-carbohydrate foods such as low-sugar breakfast cereals, bread and beans provide sustained energy and help to keep blood sugar levels on an even keel. Recent research suggests that children who eat a carbohydrate-based breakfast are likely to perform better at school.

School lunches vary in quality and choice depending on where you live, with some councils abolishing them altogether. A packed lunch may be the only way you can ensure that your child is getting nutritious food – that's as long as it's eaten! Turn to page 81 for some ideas. At this age, tea or supper may become the main meal of the day. Even if your child has a cooked school lunch, it's advisable to give him or her a decent meal in the afternoon or evening to ensure that he or she is getting a sufficient range of nutrients. Now your child is older, it may be feasible to eat communal meals. Eating together encourages children to try a wider variety of food as well as to enjoy the social aspect of sharing mealtimes.

Junk foods

There are very few completely 'bad' foods, but there are many which are best avoided – those containing E numbers and other additives, artificial colourings, sweeteners, hydrogenated and saturated fat, as well as excessively sugary and salty foods. Poor-quality foods, including cheap biscuits, cakes, processed meats

ABOVE *A good breakfast before a day at school is vital to keep energy levels high, and stops your child snacking.*

and cheeses, pies, sugary fizzy drinks and packet desserts are just some of the foods that fall into this category.

We all buy convenience foods, but do try to opt for fish fingers containing the highest percentage of fish, sausages and pies with a high meat content, jam with a high fruit content and biscuits, cakes and cereals that are lower in sugar than others. Better still, it really is worth taking the time to make your own versions and ensure that fruit or vegetables play an important part.

• To make healthier chips: cut potatoes into wedges, retaining the skin, then brush with olive oil and bake in the oven. Good source of vitamin C and fibre.

• Top a pizza base with home-made tomato sauce, grated cheese and vegetables. Good source of vitamin C, beta-carotene and calcium.

• Use lean meat and grated vegetables to make home-made burgers. Combine mashed beans and grated vegetables to make a vegetarian alternative. Brush the burgers with oil and grill. Good source of iron, vitamins C and B.

• Make a healthier version of a 'knickerbocker glory' with natural yogurt or good-quality ice cream, fresh fruit purée and chopped toasted nuts. Pile high in a glass. A good source of vitamins B, C and calcium.

MEAL PLANNER 7

4+ YEARS	BREAKFAST	LUNCH	TEA	SUPPER
Day 1	Porridge and dried apricots Toast	Wiggly noodle soup with chicken/ tofu/prawns, Fromage frais OR packed/school lunch	Sunny rice, green vegetables Buttermilk pancakes with hot maple bananas	Sandwich, fruit Milky drink
Day 2	Boiled egg, toast, banana	Chicken, apple & nut salad, bread Baked apple & custard OR packed/school lunch	Green giant pasta Garlic bread Sponge sandcastles	Muffin/scone Fruit Milky drink
Day 3	Cereal, toasted fruit bread	Chinese omelette roll, yogurt OR packed/school lunch	Honey salmon kebabs, rice and vegetables Passion cake squares	Crackers & cheese Apple & grapes Milky drink
Day 4	Toasted bacon and tomato sandwich, yogurt	Bean & pasta soup Tortilla parcel Strawberry & vanilla ice OR packed/school lunch	Mini burger & bun Sweet potato wedges Grated carrot Baked peach crumbles	Sardines on toast Fruit Milky drink
Day 5	Cereal, toast, melon	Creamy smoked salmon & broccoli pasta Fresh fruit sticks OR packed/school lunch	Winter sausage hot pot, vegetables Fromage frais	Gingerbread person Fruit Milky drink
Day 6	Bubble & squeak cakes Grilled tomatoes Fresh orange juice	Spicy rice balls with tomato sauce Crispy chicken fingers Ice cream sundae	Pork & apple casserole Potatoes & vegetables Chocolate bread pudding	Malt loaf Fruit Milky drink
Day 7	Scrambled egg Kipper & toast	Christmas pie Roast potatoes & vegetables Little Jack Horner pudding	Tomato & lentil soup Pizza fingers Banana custard scrunch	Sandwich Fruit Milky drink

Lunchbox Ideas

Many of us get stuck in a rut when it comes to providing interesting and varied lunchboxes everyday – it's all too easy to stick to the usual sandwich, crisps, yogurt and apple. Time is also at a premium in the morning, when preparing a lunchbox has to be juggled with breakfast, getting dressed and the school run. The following ideas will hopefully inspire and most can be prepared ahead of time, so they shouldn't demand too much attention when time is against you. By varying your daily offering, you add an element of surprise and hopefully your efforts will pay off – there's nothing more frustrating than when a lunchbox returns home with its contents untouched.

Mini Pasties

PREPARATION TIME: 10 MINUTES PLUS 15 MINUTES SOAKING	
COOKING TIME: 35 MINUTES **FREEZING:** SUITABLE **SERVES:** 6	

These mini pasties make a great addition to a lunchbox or picnic and are the right size for toddlers to hold. They can also be served warm for supper with new potatoes and vegetables. The flaky puff-pastry triangles encase a rich mixture of soya mince (or lean beef mince) and vegetables.

❶ Put the soya mince in a bowl and cover with boiling water. Add the yeast extract and stir until dissolved. Leave the soya for 15 minutes, until rehydrated. Meanwhile, steam or boil the potatoes and carrots until tender.

❷ Heat the oil in a pan and sauté the onion for 5 minutes. Add the garlic and sauté for a further minute, stirring occasionally, until the onion has softened.

❸ Add the cooked carrot and potato, the parsley, soya mince (and any soaking liquid), passata and soy sauce to the pan. Stir thoroughly, season with pepper to taste, and cook for 10 minutes.

❹ Preheat the oven to 200°C/400°F/Gas Mark 6. Place the pastry on a work surface and cut into 6 x 10-cm/4-in squares. Place a heaped teaspoon of the filling in the centre of each pastry square. Brush the edges with the beaten egg and fold the pastry in half to make a triangle. Seal the edges with a fork, then repeat to make 5 more pasties.

❺ Place the pasties on a lightly greased baking sheet, brush with the remaining egg and make a small air hole in the top using a skewer. Bake for 15–20 minutes, or until risen and golden.

INGREDIENTS:
25 g/1 oz dried soya mince (look for one that is GM free)
½ tsp yeast extract
1 small potato, peeled and diced
1 small carrot, peeled and diced
1 tsp vegetable oil
1 small onion, finely chopped
1 clove garlic, crushed
1 tbsp finely chopped fresh parsley
2 tbsp passata
1 tbsp soy sauce
freshly ground black pepper
375 g/13 oz ready-rolled puff pastry, defrosted if frozen
1 egg, beaten, to glaze

Guacamole

PREPARATION TIME: 5 MINUTES	
FREEZING: UNSUITABLE	SERVES: 2–4

This creamy dip is simple to prepare and makes a great filling for warm tortillas, pitta bread or sandwiches. Although the lemon juice helps the avocado to retain its colour, the guacamole is best eaten within a few hours of making.

❶ Place the avocado in a bowl and add the lemon juice, garlic and tomato (if using). Mash with a fork until smooth and creamy.

INGREDIENTS:
1 ripe avocado, peeled, stoned and roughly chopped
juice of ½ lemon
1 small clove garlic, crushed
1 tomato, skinned, seeded and diced (optional)

Fishy Pasta Salad

PREPARATION TIME: 5 MINUTES	COOKING TIME: 10 MINUTES
FREEZING: UNSUITABLE	SERVES: 2–4

There is now a plethora of different pasta shapes to choose from, which adds to the fun and the appeal of this quick and easy salad. Use the prawns or salmon only if the salad can be refrigerated prior to lunchtime. If not, add diced red pepper and halved black grapes, which taste just as good.

❶ Cook the pasta according to the instructions on the packet, until tender, then drain well.

❷ Mix together the mayonnaise and ketchup in a bowl and add the pasta, prawns and tomatoes. Line a container with lettuce leaves and spoon the pasta salad into the middle.

INGREDIENTS:
85 g/3 oz pasta shapes of your choice
2 tbsp mayonnaise
1 tbsp tomato ketchup
55 g/2 oz cooked prawns or canned pink salmon, mashed (optional)
3 cherry tomatoes, quartered
lettuce leaves, optional

Cheese Twists

PREPARATION TIME: 5 MINUTES **COOKING TIME:** 12 MINUTES

FREEZING: SUITABLE **SERVES:** 20 TWISTS

These savoury twists have a delicious cheesy flavour and are very tasty. They can be dipped into houmus.

❶ Preheat the oven to 200°C/400°F/Gas Mark 6. Grease a large baking sheet.

❷ Mix together the Gruyère cheese and paprika and sprinkle over the sheet of puff pastry. Fold the puff pastry in half and roll out a little to seal the edges.

❸ Cut the pastry into long 1-cm/ ½-in wide strips, then cut each strip in half and gently twist. Place on the prepared baking sheet. Brush with beaten egg and bake for 10–12 minutes, or until crisp and golden. Allow the cheese twists to cool on a wire rack.

INGREDIENTS:
butter or margarine, for greasing
85 g/3 oz Gruyère cheese, grated
½ tsp paprika
375 g/13 oz ready-rolled puff pastry, defrosted if frozen
1 egg, beaten

Sandwiches

- Bagel with cream cheese and yeast extract
- Peanut butter with strawberry jam
- Peanut butter with mashed banana
- Sliced cooked chicken with grated apple and mayonnaise
- Chicken and mashed banana
- Mashed tuna, avocado with mayonnaise and a squeeze of lemon juice
- Houmus, diced tomato and chopped hard-boiled egg
- Sliced grilled bacon, chopped hard-boiled egg and mayonnaise
- Ham, mashed pineapple chunks and cottage cheese
- Cheese scones with bacon and cream cheese
- Vegetarian sausages with tomato
- Ciabatta with a wedge of omelette

- Ciabatta with pesto, mozzarella cheese and tomato
- Sardine paté and cucumber
- Pitta bread with couscous, houmus and mint
- Pitta bread pizzas

Snacks

- Raisin muffins with cream cheese
- Rice cakes with chocolate spread and sliced banana
- Nuts and raisins
- Breadsticks and dip
- Crumpets with strawberry jam and cream cheese
- Mini pitta breads spread with garlic butter and sprinkled with grated cheese and grilled
- Tortilla
- Flapjacks
- Malt loaf or fruit bread
- Fruit jelly with fresh fruit
- Houmus with sticks of carrot, cucumber and celery

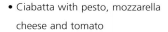

Lemon Barley Water

PREPARATION TIME: 5 MINUTES **COOKING TIME:** 35 MINUTES	
FREEZING: SUITABLE **SERVES:** 1.7 LITRES/3 PINTS	

This homemade lemon drink is very refreshing on a hot day and is great for when your child has friends to play. It has less sugar than many shop-bought versions.

❶ Rinse the barley under cold running water, then place in a large saucepan. Cover with water and bring to the boil. Reduce the heat and simmer for 30 minutes, skimming off any froth that may appear from time to time. Remove the pan from the heat.

❷ Add the lemon rind and sugar to the pan, stir well until the sugar has dissolved and leave to cool. Strain, then add the lemon juice. Chill.

INGREDIENTS:
225 g/8 oz pearl barley
1.7 litres/3 pints water
grated rind of 1 lemon
55 g/2 oz golden caster sugar
juice of 2 lemons

VARIATION Substitute orange rind and juice for the lemon rind and juice for a different flavour.

Strawberry & Banana Shake

PREPARATION TIME: 5 MINUTES	
FREEZING: SUITABLE **SERVES:** 2	

This creamy fruity drink can be transformed into delicious lollies if it is frozen. You can use other fruit combinations too.

❶ Put the bananas, strawberries, wheatgerm and yogurt in a blender and process for a minute, or until the mixture is smooth and creamy. Pour into tall glasses and serve with coloured straws.

INGREDIENTS:
2 bananas, quartered
225 g/8 oz strawberries, hulled and halved if large
1 tbsp wheatgerm or oatmeal
500 g/1 lb 2 oz natural live yogurt

Wiggly Noodle Soup

PREPARATION TIME: 5 MINUTES   **COOKING TIME:** 8 MINUTES

FREEZING: SUITABLE   **SERVES:** 4

Quick, nutritious and fun, this soup can be messy, so be prepared! Miso is made from soya beans, which can be bought in paste form, although here I've gone for convenience and opted for instant miso soup.

❶ Bring a large pan of water to the boil, add the noodles and cook according to the instructions on the packet, until the noodles are just tender. Drain the noodles in a colander. Rinse under cold running water, then drain again and set aside.

❷ Put the miso soup in a large saucepan and bring to the boil, then add the soy sauce.

❸ Reduce the heat and add the mangetout, carrot and spring onions, if using, and simmer for 3 minutes, or until the vegetables are just tender.

❹ Divide the noodles between four bowls and pour in the soup. Sprinkle with the sesame seeds.

INGREDIENTS:
200 g/7 oz egg noodles
1 litre/1¾ pints instant miso soup
1 tbsp dark soy sauce
115 g/4 oz mangetout, thinly sliced diagonally
1 carrot, peeled and cut into fine strips
2 spring onions, finely sliced (optional)
1 tbsp toasted sesame seeds (optional)
salt and freshly ground black pepper

Honey Salmon Kebabs

PREPARATION TIME: 5 MINUTES PLUS 1 HOUR MARINATING

COOKING TIME: 5 MINUTES   **FREEZING:** UNSUITABLE   **SERVES:** 4

The honey-based marinade gives a wonderful, sweet, caramel flavour and glossy coating to the cubes of salmon. While kebabs are fun, do take care when giving them to children. Soak wooden skewers in water to stop them burning.

❶ Mix together the ingredients for the marinade in a shallow dish. Add the salmon and stir to coat the fish in the marinade. Leave to marinate in the refrigerator for 1 hour, turning the fish occasionally.

❷ Preheat the grill to high. Thread the cubes of salmon onto 4–6 skewers. Line a grill rack with foil and place the skewers on top. Brush the salmon with the marinade and grill for 3–5 minutes, turning the skewers occasionally, until cooked.

❸ While the salmon is cooking, put the remaining marinade in a small saucepan and heat for a few minutes until it has reduced.

❹ Serve the kebabs with rice. Spoon the reduced marinade over the salmon and sprinkle with sesame seeds, if using.

INGREDIENTS:
140 g/5 oz salmon steak skinned and cut into 2-cm/¾-in cubes
1 tbsp toasted sesame seeds (optional)
MARINADE
2 tbsp runny honey
1 tbsp soy sauce
1 tbsp olive oil
1 tsp toasted sesame oil

Sunny Rice

PREPARATION TIME: 10 MINUTES	COOKING TIME: 30 MINUTES
FREEZING: SUITABLE	SERVES: 4

This comforting, lightly spiced rice dish is topped with slices of hard-boiled egg for extra goodness. Make sure you choose undyed smoked fish, not the artificially coloured variety.

INGREDIENTS:
450 g/1 lb undyed smoked haddock or cod fillets
450 ml/16 fl oz water
225 g/8 oz basmati rice, rinsed
1 bay leaf
2 cloves
4 tbsp butter
55 g/2 oz frozen petit pois
1 tsp garam masala
½ tsp ground turmeric
2 tbsp chopped flat-leaved parsley
4 hard-boiled eggs, quartered
freshly ground black pepper

❶ Put the haddock in a large frying pan and pour enough milk or water to just cover it. Poach the fish for 5 minutes. Remove the haddock from the pan and flake the fish, carefully removing the skin and any bones. Discard the poaching liquid.

❷ Meanwhile, place the rice in a saucepan and cover with 475 ml/ 16 fl oz water, then add the bay leaf and cloves. Bring to the boil, then reduce the heat and simmer for 15 minutes, or until the water has been absorbed and the rice is tender. Discard the bay leaf and cloves. Set aside the covered pan.

❸ Melt the butter over a gentle heat in the cleaned frying pan, then add the peas and cook for 2 minutes, or until tender. Stir in the garam masala and turmeric and cook for 1 minute.

❹ Stir in the haddock and rice and mix well until they are coated.

❺ Season and heat through for 1–2 minutes. Stir in the parsley and top with the hard-boiled eggs.

Chicken, Apple & Nut Salad

PREPARATION TIME: 5 MINUTES	COOKING TIME: 1 MINUTE
FREEZING: UNSUITABLE	SERVES: 2

The creamy dressing and the sweetness of the apple add to the child-appeal of this crunchy salad. I've included spring onion, but you can easily leave it out.

❶ Toast the pine kernels in a dry frying pan until lightly golden.

❷ Toss the apple in the lemon juice to prevent the flesh from discolouring. Place the apple and any leftover lemon juice in a bowl with the chicken, celery and spring onion, if using. Add the toasted pine kernels.

INGREDIENTS:
1 tbsp pine kernels
1 red-skinned apple, cored and diced
1 tbsp lemon juice
175 g/6 oz cooked chicken breast, skinned and diced
1 celery stick, finely chopped
1 spring onion, finely chopped (optional)
DRESSING
2 tbsp mayonnaise
3 tbsp natural yogurt

❸ Mix together the mayonnaise and yogurt and spoon the dressing over the salad. Mix well to coat the salad in the dressing.

Christmas Pie

PREPARATION TIME: 10 MINUTES **COOKING TIME:** 25 MINUTES
FREEZING: SUITABLE **SERVES:** 4

These individual golden puff-pastry pies are full of the flavours that are reminiscent of the festive season.

❶ Preheat the oven to 200°C/ 400°F/Gas Mark 6. Lay out the pastry on a lightly floured work surface or board. Divide the pastry into four pieces.

❷ Season the turkey breasts and cut each one into two. Arrange the turkey fillets on top of the pastry, leaving a border around the edge, then spoon over the chutney. Divide the stuffing in four and place on top.

❸ Fold the long edges of the pastry together and seal the top with water, then fold in the ends and seal. Repeat with the remaining three parcels. Cut any remaining

INGREDIENTS:
375 g/13 oz ready-rolled puff pastry, defrosted if frozen
2 skinless turkey breasts, each weighing about 115 g/4 oz
2 tbsp redcurrant chutney or cranberry jelly
150 g/5½ oz sage and onion stuffing
1 egg, beaten
salt and freshly ground black pepper

pastry into holly shapes and place on top of each parcel. Brush each pie with beaten egg and place on a lightly greased baking sheet.

❹ Bake for 25 minutes, or until the pastry is golden and the turkey done.

Baby Burgers

PREPARATION TIME: 10 MINUTES **COOKING TIME:** 20 MINUTES
FREEZING: SUITABLE **SERVES:** 10 BURGERS

There's something very appealing about bite-sized foods and these mini burgers are no exception, fitting perfectly into those sesame or poppy seed baby rolls you can now buy. These burgers are perfect for little hands to hold.

❶ Place all the ingredients for the burgers, except the oil, in a large bowl and mix together with your hands until combined. Season, then shape the mixture into small balls, using your hands. Set aside in the refrigerator for 15 minutes.

❷ Heat enough oil to cover the bottom of a large heavy-based frying pan and fry the meatballs, for 3–5 minutes, until cooked through and browned.

❸ Serve the burgers in a small bun with lettuce, sliced tomato and relish.

INGREDIENTS:
40 g/1½ oz fresh wholemeal breadcrumbs
1 tsp dried oregano
1 onion, grated
1 carrot, peeled and grated
1 clove garlic, crushed
425 g/15 oz lean beef mince
1 tbsp tomato purée
1 egg, beaten
vegetable oil, for frying
salt and freshly ground black pepper
TO SERVE
mini burger buns
lettuce leaves
sliced tomato
mayonnaise or relish

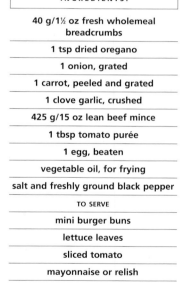

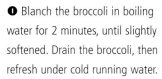

Chinese Omelette Roll

PREPARATION TIME: 5 MINUTES	**COOKING TIME:** 8 MINUTES
FREEZING: UNSUITABLE	**SERVES:** 4

A thin, golden omelette makes a remarkably good wrapping for stir-fried vegetables.

INGREDIENTS:
115 g/4 oz broccoli florets, cut into small pieces
2 tbsp groundnut oil
1 clove garlic
1-cm/½-in piece of fresh root ginger, finely grated
1 small red pepper, seeded and diced
85 g/3 oz white cabbage, finely shredded
85 g/3 oz beansprouts
2 tbsp black bean sauce
4 eggs, lightly beaten
salt and freshly ground black pepper

❶ Blanch the broccoli in boiling water for 2 minutes, until slightly softened. Drain the broccoli, then refresh under cold running water.

❷ Heat half the oil in a wok or frying pan. Add the garlic, ginger, red pepper, cabbage and broccoli and stir-fry for 3 minutes, tossing the vegetables constantly to prevent them sticking.

❸ Add the beansprouts and stir-fry for a further minute, then add the black bean sauce, stir and heat through. Remove from the heat and cover the wok or pan to keep the stir-fry warm.

❹ Season the beaten eggs. Heat a little of the remaining oil in a small frying pan and add a quarter of the beaten egg. Swirl the egg to cover the base of the pan. Cook until set, then turn the omelette out on to a plate and keep warm while you make three more omelettes.

❺ Spoon the vegetable stir-fry along the centre of the omelette and roll it up. Cut it crossways.

Green Giant Pasta

PREPARATION TIME: 10 MINUTES	**COOKING TIME:** 15 MINUTES
FREEZING: SUITABLE	**SERVES:** 4

I've included a recipe for fresh pesto, but the ready-made variety can be used if preferred or if time is short.

❶ First make the pesto. Place the basil, garlic and pine kernels in a blender and process until finely chopped. Gradually add the oil and then the Parmesan cheese and blend to a coarse purée. Season to taste. Spoon the pesto into a jar with a lid. Pour over extra olive oil to cover. Use immediately or store in the refrigerator for up to a week.

❷ Cook the pasta according to the instructions on the packet, until the pasta is just tender, then drain, reserving 1–2 tablespoons of the cooking water.

❸ Meanwhile, cook the potatoes in boiling water for 10 minutes, or until tender. Cut the potato into cubes.

❹ Heat the oil in a large saucepan, then add 4 tablespoons of pesto, the cooked potatoes and peas. Heat the pesto mixture for a few minutes, then season to taste. Add the pasta and the reserved cooking water if it

INGREDIENTS:
55 g/2 oz fresh basil leaves
2 cloves garlic, crushed
40 g/1½ oz pine kernels
125 ml/4 fl oz olive oil, plus extra for drizzling
4 tbsp freshly grated Parmesan cheese
salt and freshly ground black pepper
375 g/13 oz linguine, spaghetti or tagliatelle
8 new potatoes, halved or quartered, if large
2 tsp olive oil
55 g/2 oz frozen petit pois
1–2 tbsp pine kernels, toasted in a dry frying pan

appears too dry. Heat through and mix in the pine kernels.

❺ Serve sprinkled with cheese.

Fresh Fruit Sticks

PREPARATION TIME: 10 MINUTES	**COOKING TIME:** 15 MINUTES
FREEZING: UNSUITABLE	**SERVES:** 4

Children can help to assemble these colourful, vitamin-rich fruit sticks, but they do need adult supervision if they are very young. The fruit sticks can be grilled or barbecued and are excellent served with a dollop of thick natural yogurt or a good-quality vanilla ice cream. Wooden skewers are preferable, but do soak them for 10 minutes beforehand to prevent them burning.

❶ Preheat the grill to high and line the grill pan with foil. Arrange the fruit along the wooden skewers.

❷ Heat the honey or maple syrup in a small saucepan until it becomes runny and liquid. Brush the mixture liberally over the kebabs using a pastry brush or your fingers, if you prefer.

INGREDIENTS:
Choose from a selection of fresh fruit: pineapples, mangoes, bananas, kiwi, peaches and oranges are best, cut into 1-cm/½-in chunks
runny honey or maple syrup, for brushing

❸ Grill for 5–8 minutes, or until the fruit softens and the honey or syrup begins to caramelise.

Little Jack Horner Pudding

PREPARATION TIME: 10 MINUTES	**COOKING TIME:** 30 MINUTES
FREEZING: UNSUITABLE	**SERVES:** 4

This warming plum batter pudding is similar to the classic French dessert clafoutis. It is best served hot with cream.

❶ Preheat the oven to 200°C/400°F/Gas Mark 6.

❷ Beat the eggs, egg yolk and sugar in a large bowl until light and frothy. Stir in the vanilla essence and flour with a wooden spoon and beat until smooth.

❸ Mix together the melted butter, soured cream and milk and add to the bowl. Gently stir until everything is combined.

❹ Arrange the plums in the bottom of a lightly buttered 20 cm/8 in

INGREDIENTS:
2 eggs
1 egg yolk
85 g/3 oz caster sugar
1 tsp vanilla essence
55 g/2 oz plain flour, sifted
40 g/1½ oz unsalted butter, melted, plus extra for greasing
100 ml/3½ fl oz soured cream
50 ml/2 fl oz full-cream milk
3 plums, stoned and roughly chopped

ovenproof dish, then pour the egg mixture over the fruit. Bake for 25–30 minutes, or until the topping has risen and set.

Gingerbread People

PREPARATION TIME: 10 MINUTES   **COOKING TIME:** 12 MINUTES

FREEZING: UNSUITABLE   **SERVES:** SIX OR MORE DEPENDING ON SIZE OF CUTTER

Children love helping to make these golden gingerbread men and women and decorating them too.

❶ Preheat the oven to 190°C/375°F/Gas Mark 5. Sift the flour, ginger and bicarbonate of soda into a large mixing bowl. Add the butter and rub into the flour with your fingers until the mixture resembles fine breadcrumbs. Mix in the sugar.

❷ Warm the syrup in a small saucepan until runny, then add to the flour mixture with the beaten egg. Mix to form a soft dough, then knead until smooth. If the dough is too sticky, add a little extra flour.

INGREDIENTS:
175 g/6 oz plain flour
2 tsp ground ginger
½ tsp bicarbonate of soda
55 g/2 oz butter or margarine
85 g/3 oz soft brown sugar
2 tbsp golden syrup
1 egg, beaten
to decorate
Royal icing, piping consistency
Smarties or raisins

❸ Roll out the dough on a lightly floured work surface then, using a cutter, make the gingerbread people. Place on a lightly greased baking sheet and cook for 10 minutes, or until just crisp and golden. Allow to cool.

❹ Pipe small blobs of icing to make a face and buttons on each person. Use the Smarties or raisins to form eyes and buttons.

Passion Cake Squares

PREPARATION TIME: 15 MINUTES   **COOKING TIME:** 1 HOUR

FREEZING: SUITABLE, WITHOUT ICING   **MAKES:** 16–20 SQUARES

This moist, light carrot cake couldn't be easier to make and is a delicious way to encourage your child to eat vegetables!

❶ Preheat the oven to 180°C/ 350°F/Gas Mark 4. Lightly grease a 20-cm/8-in square cake tin and line the base with greaseproof paper.

❷ Sift the flour and salt into a large mixing bowl. Add the spices, sugar, carrots and dates and mix well.

❸ Stir together the beaten eggs and oil, then pour into the mixing bowl and beat until thoroughly combined.

❹ Pour the slightly lumpy mixture into the prepared tin and bake for 1 hour, or until a skewer inserted into the centre of the cake comes out clean. Leave for 5 minutes, then carefully turn out the cake and cool.

❺ To make the icing, beat the cream cheese, butter and vanilla essence together until smooth and creamy. Beat in the sugar and store the icing in the refrigerator for 20 minutes to harden slightly. Spread the icing over the cake and cut into small squares.

INGREDIENTS:
225 g/8 oz self-raising flour
pinch of salt
1 tsp ground cinnamon
1 tsp ground nutmeg
225 g/8 oz light muscovado sugar
225 g/8 oz carrots, peeled and finely grated
100 g/3½ oz dried, ready-to-eat dates, roughly chopped
3 eggs, lightly beaten
175 ml/6 fl oz sunflower oil
icing
115 g/4 oz cream cheese
4 tbsp butter
1 tsp vanilla essence
200 g/7 oz icing sugar

Useful Websites and Organisations

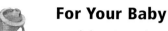

For Your Baby

www.babycentre.co.uk
The UK's hands-on guide to pregnancy, birth and life.

www.kidshealth.org
Large sections on 'Feeding your newborn,' 'Feeding your 1–3 month old,' 'Feeding your 4–7 month old' and 'Feeding your 8–12 month old'. Plus useful question and answer sections, detailing topics you might have queries about, and the usual chat rooms for informal research.

www.babyworld.co.uk
Good information on what first foods to offer between 4 to 6 months; feeding from 6 to 9 months; feeding from 12 months on; food intolerances and common food allergies; vegetarian babies; vegan babies; special diets; vitamin supplements; organic baby foods tried and tested and some baby recipes to try.

www.parenthood.com
General information on coping with your newborn and the right time to introduce solids.

babyparenting.about.com
A selection of recipes for first foods and information on breastfeeding your newborn.

www.babycenter.com
Information on health and development, breastfeeding, introducing first foods and nutritional guides.

www.parenttime.com
Chat forums you can visit to discuss any questions you may have with other parents, and a chance to gather information and raise any queries and questions of your own about newborns.

Association of Breastfeeding Mothers
Email: abm@clara.net
www.abm.me.uk
Offers breastfeeding advice and information, and trains breastfeeding counsellors.

Centre for Pregnancy Nutrition
pregnancy.nutrition@sheffield.ac.uk
Helpline: (+44) 0114 2424084

For Your Toddler

www.kidsource.com
Addresses health and diseases issues, and the correct kind of preventive care. Also deals with nutritional questions.

www.drgreene.com/toddlers.html
Information on the effect of sugar on behaviour and the value of vegetables – plus advice on handling temper tantrums.

www.forparentsbyparents.com
This UK parenting site is funded, founded and maintained by parents. The site aims to give an honest view of parenting, even the grim bits!

www.parentingtoddlers.com
Practical advice and tips on parenting toddlers.

kidshealth.org
A useful site with sections on feeding your toddler: feeding your 1–2 year old, deciphering food labels, healthy mealtime habits, nutrients your child needs and packing school lunches.

www.allhealth.com
This site gives information on school-age nutrition, an area that often worries parents because their children come under different influences when they start full-time education.

Fathers Direct
www.fathersdirect.com
Email: mail@fathersdirect.com
Promotes close and positive relationships between men and their children from infancy. Aims to break down barriers that exist in society that make it difficult for fathers to develop such relationships with their children.

Parentline Plus
www.parentline.co.uk
Helpline: (+44) 0808 800 2222
Offers support to anyone who is parenting a child – the child's parents, step-parents, grandparents and foster parents. Provides a range of information.

Index

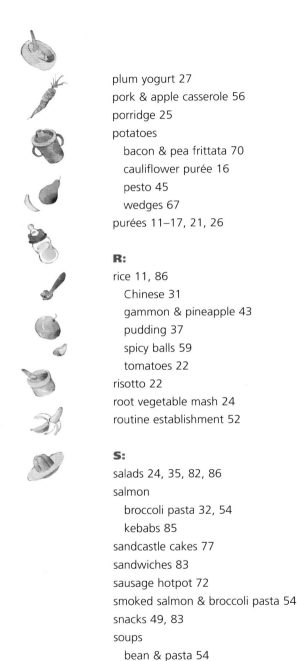

plum yogurt 27
pork & apple casserole 56
porridge 25
potatoes
    bacon & pea frittata 70
    cauliflower purée 16
    pesto 45
    wedges 67
purées 11–17, 21, 26

R:
rice 11, 86
    Chinese 31
    gammon & pineapple 43
    pudding 37
    spicy balls 59
    tomatoes 22
risotto 22
root vegetable mash 24
routine establishment 52

S:
salads 24, 35, 82, 86
salmon
    broccoli pasta 32, 54
    kebabs 85
sandcastle cakes 77
sandwiches 83
sausage hotpot 72
smoked salmon & broccoli pasta 54
snacks 49, 83
soups
    bean & pasta 54
    lentil & tomato 66
    minestrone 21

noodle 85
tomato 44, 66
spicy rice balls 59
spinach & French bean purée 17
sponge pudding 46
spring vegetable risotto 22
starfish pie 57
strawberry
    banana milkshakes 84
    ice cream sundae 75
    vanilla yogurt ice 60
    yogurt lollies 47
summer pudding 46
sundaes 36, 75
sunny rice 86
sunset jelly 27
swede & apricot purée 16
sweet potato wedges 67

T:
toast, cinnamon 36
tomatoes
    bean pie 73
    lentil soup 66
    rice 22
    sauce 33, 59
    soup 44, 66

tortilla parcels 74
tuna
    pasta 44
    salad 24
turkey, Christmas pie 87

V:
vegetables
    chickpea curry 41
    crudités
    mash 24
    pasta cheese 32
    purées 11–17, 21
    risotto 22
    see also individual vegetables

W:
weaning guidelines 7, 9
websites 91

Y:
yogurts 26–7
    lollies 47
    strawberry & vanilla ice 60

Acknowledgements

The publisher would like to thank the following for permission
to reproduce copyright material:
Bridgewater Book Company: p. 7; Bubbles: pp. 29, 50, 63, 64, 79;
Getty Stone: pp. 38, 50, 51; Image Bank: pp. 4, 5, 6, 8, 18, 19, 28, 39,
48, 49, 62, 78; Superstock: pp. 6, 48.